GLEN HANSON

W9-BSR-701

Smart Money
Real Estate
for the 80s

Smart Money
Real Estate
for the 80s

New Profits in Big Properties

Robert Irwin

**Published in San Francisco by
HARBOR PUBLISHING**

Distributed by G. P. Putnam's Sons

Copyright © 1982 by Robert Irwin
All rights reserved.

No part of this book may be reproduced in any form or by any
means, electronic or mechanical, including photocopy, recording,
or any information storage and retrieval system, without
permission in writing from the publisher.

For information contact Harbor Publishing,
1668 Lombard Street, San Francisco, CA 94123.

Printed in the United States of America.

Composition and design: Printed Page Graphics
Copyeditor: Russell Fuller
Text printer & binder: Fairfield Graphics
Cover design: Hal Lockwood, Bookman Productions

ISBN: 0-936602-41-4

NOTE TO READER

The investment opinions expressed in this book are strictly those of the
author. Because of the myriad financial situations in which individuals
find themselves, no guarantee or assurance is given that following any
of the material in this book will lead to a successful investment. For
legal, tax, and investment advice on a particular property, you should
consult with your own attorney or personal financial advisor.

For Jack

CONTENTS

INTRODUCTION

How can you find the right investment in the troubled waters of today's economy? Besides holding your money in treasury bills or money-market accounts, how are you going to invest in a way that makes good sense? How can you begin to accumulate money without taking unacceptable risks? How do you get from where you are today to financial freedom tomorrow? We all know it's a real problem. Yesterday's answers won't work anymore.

In the past, many of us bought stocks and bonds. But, the stock market has performed terribly in the recent past, and the bond market had dipped down to touch forty-year lows. Many people invested in precious metals, such as gold and silver, or in rare items such as coins, stamps, or paintings. But, the first years of this decade have taught us that these investments can drop in value just as fast as they can rise. As of this writing, gold has lost more than half the value it achieved in 1980; silver has lost more than four-fifths! Collectibles are stagnating, with prices falling lower and lower. An investor who buys here can only hope to hold on for the long term . . . and pray.

Investing in homes was perhaps the richest, most popular investment of the last five years. "Just buy a house, any house; hold it for six months and you can double your money!" Who said that? I did! In several popular books, I exhorted people to get on the bandwagon in time to take advantage of the housing boom. But, as housing foreclosures and failing prices demonstrate, that time is past. The day when you could throw a dollar at a housing investment and have ten come flying back is over.

Well then, why not give up "investing"? Why not just leave our money in money-market accounts and treasury bills (T-bills)? With high interest rates, T-bills and other government-insured securities are certainly the most secure of all possible investments. They are virtually risk-free. The problem is that their profit potential is limited—in most times, they pay only a few percentage points above the rate of inflation. As most financial advisors point out, T-bills, money-market accounts and so on are terrific places to *hold* your money while you're waiting for a good investment. But, they should not be confused with a good investment. As we'll see in our chapter on evaluation, you want both a return *on* your money and a return *of* your money. When the return of and on your money is considered in inflated dollars *after taxes*, most money-market accounts and T-bills are lucky to break even.

When the answers of the past don't work, where do we turn to find good investments today? As I said, finding a place to invest our money can seem impossible.

But it is possible. First of all, we have to make some different assumptions about the times in which we live. During the early to mid-1980s, we probably are going to be living in a period of severe recession to mild expansion. That means that the boom days of overnight profits won't be around again for a while. If we're smart, we'll realize that we can't afford to buy in this economic climate, if we're counting on a profitable quick sale. Secondly, we'll see that some smart people right next to us are prospering in today's economic climate. We need to find out how they're making their money and see if we can do the same.

Those are the two key elements to financial freedom in the mid-1980s: (1) learning to be smart with our money, and (2) finding out where the smart money is being invested.

This book offers an answer to both questions—an answer you may not have considered before, because you felt you hadn't enough capital or sufficient experience, or because you just never thought about it. This book asks you to consider "investment real estate" as a smart way to invest your money, and as the place where the smart money is going.

What is "investment real estate"?

Obviously, I'm not talking about buying a home to rent and then resell. I'm dealing with what most people call *big* real estate. I'm speaking of shopping centers, office buildings, industrial parks, mobile home parks and more. I'm talking about real estate especially suited to investors and investment.

Why is it smart to go into investment real estate today? Let's consider risks and rewards.

On the risk side, investment real estate offers the opportunity to get in very often with relatively little cash. The amount you have "at risk" can be smaller here than in many other types of investment. In addition, if investment real estate is well purchased, it has "staying power." If times get bad, and you purchased correctly, you can hang onto the investment until times get better.

On the reward side, many areas of investment real estate are now booming. Yes—at the same time that the housing market is in near collapse—office buildings, commercial centers, industrial buildings and others are showing rapid appreciation in many areas. Many people are quite surprised to learn this. They have been hearing news on radio, television and in print about the collapse of the real estate market. They hear that prices have leveled off or even fallen in many areas, and that building is half of what it was the previous year.

It is important to understand that, ninety-nine percent of the time, the media reports only on the *housing market*. While housing is indeed the largest single share of the real estate market, it is not the only share. Investment real estate is also extremely large. When housing is crashing, it does not follow that investment real estate is doing likewise. The two markets frequently work at opposition to each other—when one is going down, the other may be going up. This is a vital point to grasp. The big returns possible today in investment real estate are, of course, the reason that the "smart money" already is moving into the area.

Think of all the reasons you or others went into housing

during the last five years—rapid price appreciation, tax benefits, available financing, etc. These advantages are still available
today in many types of investment real estate, and, in the area
of tax benefits, the advantages have been sharply increased by
the 1981 Economic Recovery Tax Act (ERTA). It's not hard to
see why the smart money increasingly is turning to investment
real estate.

But what about your money? I've heard people say, "It's too
big for me. I don't know anything about it." When I ask these
same people what they knew about residential real estate
before they bought their first house, they almost always reply,
"Nothing." Then I tell them that investment real estate isn't
any different. You learn as you go along.

I still see them shaking their heads, and I can hear them
thinking to themselves, "That's *big* real estate—I can't touch
that." At that point, I like to refer to the old saying, "You never
know until you try." Try it. You might find that you really can
do it, and that you enjoy it.

Of course, many books have suggested how to get started
in real estate, and, almost without exception, they point to
housing. They tell the reader how to get in for nothing down;
how to get 110 percent financing; how to find an old, run-down
building, fix it up, and sell for a profit. None of these popular
books, however, breaks the mold and talks about today's real
world. As we'll see in the second chapter, houses may *not* be
a good investment option for you or anyone today. The profits
may be over for a while, the management headaches multiplying. In today's market, you can lose money buying a house,
even a fixer-upper.

The book you're holding is unique. I'm not telling you to go
into houses. I'm telling you to stay away from them! I'm
pointing out that the opportunity is elsewhere. There's a sec-
ondary advantage here. Very few people are involved in
investment real estate, yet. Most of the investors are those who
have been here for years. There's very little new blood. Ask
your friends, who have invested in houses during the past few
years, if they've ever bought an office building, a small strip
shopping center, or an industrial park or building. If you get
any "yeses," you're traveling in a pretty sophisticated group.

In this book, it will be quite evident why the smart money is moving into investment real estate. But more than that, we'll see very clearly, through examples, how you or anyone else can get in.

This is not a simple-minded book. I'm going to assume that you know a few basics—that you know what a mortgage is; that you have some knowledge of what renting and leasing involves; and that you've perhaps already owned and rented out a house. But I'll assume that you've never gotten into investment real estate before. We'll walk through the process of getting started in investment real estate: we'll see how we evaluate property; where the profit is in conversions of apartment buildings to condominiums; how to build your own strip shopping center; and when to buy an office building. The emphasis is on how to do it.

We're going to learn how to be smart with our money in real estate in the 1980s.

Chapter One

THE NEW TAX-LAW BENEFITS FOR REAL ESTATE

Real estate has always offered enormous tax benefits to the investor, but the 1981 Economic Recovery Tax Act increased those benefits substantially, making real estate an even smarter place to put your money.* When compared with other investments today, real estate truly shines in terms of tax benefits. ERTA is reason enough for you to consider investment real estate for your financial future. But, how did ERTA specifically benefit real estate? How do the new tax-law changes increase investment-property opportunities?

In chapter four we'll go into specifics on how taxation, tax shelters, depreciation, and so on work. But here, let's assume that we just want to find out how the tax benefits of ERTA have helped real property. To do that, we need to compare the way taxation in real estate is today with the way it was before ERTA.

*(Note: The benefits described here may or may not apply to your own particular investment and tax situation. Before taking any action that could have tax consequences, you should consult with your own CPA/accountant or tax attorney. This chapter, in part, was first published in the March 1982 issue of Private Practice magazine.)

DEPRECIATION

In the past, the length of time a property could be depreciated depended on various circumstances such as age and guidelines established by the government. (As investors know, depreciation is taking an annual expense for the ultimate loss in value of real property—the building, not the land. It is capitalizing that loss.) Typically, new buildings were depreciated for forty years, while used buildings were given lifespans of twenty to thirty years. The new tax law changed all that. Today the term is fixed at fifteen years (although a longer term of thirty-five or forty-five years may be elected). The effect of this change has been enormous. In many cases property can now be depreciated more than *twice* as fast as before. That means that, each year, the investor might claim more than twice as much in tax write-offs as before.

As if this nugget were not enough, the new tax law also increased the *rate* at which property could be depreciated. In the past, straight-line depreciation (taking an equal amount each year the property was depreciated) or an accelerated rate of 125 percent for used residential property (taking 125% of straight-line) was used. Under ERTA the rate for accelerated depreciation has been raised to 175 percent. For used property that's an enormous jump which further increases the depreciation write-off an investor can take.

To see the actual effect of the new law, let's consider the depreciation on a piece of property from both the old and the new rules:

OLD RULES

$100,000	property value (not including land)
÷ 25 years	old term
$ 4,000	first-year, straight-line depreciation
× 125%	old accelerated rate (residential, used)
$ 5,000	total first-year depreciation

NEW RULES

$100,000	property value (not including land)
÷ 15 years	new term
$ 6,666	straight-line depreciation
× 175%	new accelerated rate
$ 11,666	total first-year depreciation

COMPARISON OF DEPRECIATION

New Rules	$11,666
Old Rules	$ 5,000
increase	$ 6,666

Under ERTA we more than *double* the amount of depreciation. For a taxpayer who is in the fifty percent tax bracket and for whom the depreciation is all a write-off, the figures are even more dramatic:

OLD DEPRECIATION

$5,000	amount
× 50%	tax bracket
$2,500	after-tax savings

NEW DEPRECIATION

$11,666	amount
× 50%	tax bracket
$ 5,833	after-tax savings

The higher income taxpayer (50 percent bracket) can more than double his or her tax savings under ERTA in this first-year analysis.

The results of the new depreciation rules are to make many properties far more appealing to investors. Now, ERTA promises to give so much *after-tax* cash flow that the whole picture of real estate is being turned around.

RECOVERY AND RECAPTURE

There were more changes in ERTA than depreciation. Many people have missed the new rules with regard to *recovery*— what happens when you sell the property.

As most investors know, real estate is a "deferral" type of tax shelter. The write-off you get today is not "tax-free" in the sense that, for example, the interest from an all-savers' certificate is. Rather, it is tax-deferred. You write it off against your ordinary income today, but tomorrow, when you sell, you have to pay tax on it in the form of a gain.

For example, if we write off $12,000 this year, when we sell in the future we will probably show a gain of $12,000. This year we get a write-off, but next year, or when we sell, we get it back as income.

There are two advantages here. First, if this was a particularly good year and we are in a high tax bracket, we might anticipate that next year won't be quite so good and we might be in a lower bracket. By deferring $12,000 from this year's income to the future, we can hope to get it back in a year when we are in a lower bracket. This is of particular interest now that ERTA also includes tax reductions for the next several years.

Secondly, if we've held the property for more than one year (and otherwise qualify), we can take the gain when we sell as a *capital gain*. That means we'll get it at the maximum effective rate of 20 percent.

All of this is called recovery. But, there's another part of recovery that most investors don't like. It's called, *recapture*. Recapture means that a portion of our gain upon sale *won't qualify* for capital-gains treatment. Instead it will come back as ordinary income and be taxed in our ordinary tax bracket (50 percent). It's easy to see why recapture has a bad name.

The new ERTA rules provide for *full* recapture *if* you take any accelerated depreciation on nonresidential property. (But, the old rules still hold for residential property; that is, we recapture only that portion of depreciation which is the excess of straight-line over accelerated depreciation.)

CALCULATING RECAPTURE

$ 11,666	accelerated depreciation
$ −6,666	straight-line
$ 5,000	excess recaptured

If we were to sell our house after one year, that portion we depreciated as straight-line would be recovered at the more favorable capital-gains rate. But that portion which was attributable to accelerated depreciation ($5,000) would be recovered at ordinary income rates as high as 50 percent.

What's the advantage here? It looks as if ERTA has thrown us a curve. Not really, however. We still get the benefits of the shorter term. And we still can take accelerated depreciation in nonresidential and get the quick write-off and deferral into the future. What we lose is the capital-gains combination with accelerated depreciation.

With residential, of course, we get all the benefits. We can even use accelerated depreciation in residential and, in theory, never have any recapture. It all comes about because of the short, 15-year-depreciation term and how recapture is defined.

In the past no one ever considered holding their property for the full depreciation term. Who could hold it for 30 or 40 years?! Holding it for 15 years, or even 10, however, isn't that unrealistic—and what a difference that makes. Consider a 15-year holding period. Whether we use straight-line or accelerated depreciation or switch from accelerated to straight-line, two facts will always remain true: (1) we can't depreciate the building for more than it's worth ($100,000); and (2) at the end of the term (15 years), by whatever method we use, the remaining balance will be zero. At the end of the term the house will be fully depreciated by any method used.

But, if at year 15, straight-line and accelerated are *both* zero, then there is no excess of one over the other. And since recovery is defined as "the excess of straight-line over accelerated," there is nothing to recapture!

It is now possible to recover all the money depreciated at the more favorable capital-gains rate. Even if we hold our property for only ten years, because of the way accelerated depreciation works, we can still sell and have very little recapture.

Anti-Churning

A word of warning—if you already own real estate, please keep in mind that these new depreciation rules apply to property acquired after January 1, 1981. The creators of the law foresaw that some investors who already owned property might take advantage of the new rules by trading between themselves: I trade my property to you (via a 1031 tax-deferred exchange); you trade yours to me; and suddenly we each have newly acquired property and new depreciation advantages.

Unfortunately, that's not the case. There is a special provision that can prevent persons from converting pre-1981-owned real estate into property which qualifies for the recovery rules as just described. If we trade, we might have to take the old depreciation method with us into the new property. It's all part of the anti-churning provisions.

Low-Income Housing and Rehabilitations

There are, however, other advantages in ERTA. For the higher income professionals, the opportunities in low-income housing may need to be reconsidered. In low-income housing a 200 percent declining balance depreciation now can be taken, and it automatically converts to straight-line depreciation at the appropriate time. In addition, while in the past it was necessary to capitalize the construction costs for interest and taxes over the life of low-income housing, that is no longer true. They can be expensed immediately, resulting in far larger first-year write-offs. This dramatically increases the tax advantages of the so-called "deep shelters."

ERTA also offers startling benefits with regard to *rehabilitation*. As those who have invested in them know, rehabilitation projects qualify for a special short-term, five-year depreciation. The problem, however, was that the amount of rehabilitation expense which qualified for the five-year term was limited to $20,000 per unit. Now that has been changed. The new limits are $40,000 per unit, which can double the amount of write-off potential for rehabs. And, perhaps even more interesting, there are new tax credits now available.

REHAB TAX CREDITS

As most investors know, a tax credit is a wonderful thing to have. It is not a deduction to be subtracted from ordinary income. Rather, it is a credit to be directly subtracted from tax to be paid. It is a bottom-line deduction.

The new rehab tax credit is for as much as 25 percent and is limited to buildings which retain three-quarters of their existing walls but are otherwise "substantially rehabilitated and qualified." The credit is:

1. Fifteen percent for nonresidential buildings at least 30 years old.
2. Twenty percent for nonresidential buildings at least 40 years old.
3. Twenty-five percent for qualifying historic buildings.

(*Note:* Only straight-line depreciation may be claimed if the credit is to be taken. Also, the basis is reduced for depreciation purposes by the amount of credits taken.)

The new rehab credits became available after December 31, 1981.

ULTIMATE EFFECTS OF THE NEW TAX LAW

That in a nutshell is what ERTA has done for real estate (of course, there are other conditions and rules, and you should ask your CPA/accountant or tax attorney if they apply in your case), and the effects of the new law may be coming sooner than most of us expect.

Because of the tax benefits available through ERTA, many investors are now beginning to see the current market in a new light. They are seeing it not as a period of decay, but rather as one of opportunity. Soft prices mean that investors can get bargains, even steals. While ERTA has not exactly kindled a new real estate boom, for those with a keen eye and a clear understanding of what's happening, it has provided a great opportunity.

Chapter Two

WHAT'S WRONG WITH RENTAL HOUSING?

"The place to get started in real estate is to buy a house."

That's been the rule for a long, long time. But is it still the smart thing to do today? The housing market in the 1980s is generally overpriced and is failing in most areas of the country. Isn't it pretty dumb to get started in housing?

I think it can be, particularly with the opportunities available in investment real estate as we'll soon see. But first, I think it's important to understand why being smart today means taking a different approach to real estate. If you're already convinced that you should at least consider investment property, it's important now to become convinced why you should bypass the traditional starting point—the rental house.

As I write this, the state of single-family homes is static. Even in the boom areas of California and across the Sunbelt to Florida, prices have stabilized. In many cases they have declined, as evidenced by sellers having to accept paper mortgages instead of cash at the time of sale. This is not to say that the housing market will collapse or that prices will fall in half. I simply want to point out that an investor can no longer go out blindly, buy a single-family home (or condo), and expect a strong price appreciation over a few years. Yes, this may still happen in a few areas, but not in most. Only the most adroit investors will be able to take advantage of what gains there are.

REASONS FOR A COLLAPSE
OF THE HOUSING MARKET

No one knows if the housing market is going to go into a dive as it did in the 1930s. But there are at least five convincing reasons why the housing situation is in trouble today and could get worse. I liken them to fingers on a hand that has closed around the neck of the housing market and is squeezing the life out of it.

Price

The first finger of the stranglehold is the price of a single-family home or condominium.

We all know the price of homes is high. But price is only relative. In Hong Kong, for example, a family can expect to pay $300,000 for a modest home! The price in Germany or in the cities of France and Belgium might be $150,000. By comparison with a U.S. medium price of under $80,000, our homes may seem a real bargain.

However, when compared to the price of homes in the early seventies, today's prices seem very high indeed. In many areas of the country, homes are selling for as much as three times what they cost seven years ago, and we can relate far more easily to prices in our communities seven years ago than to today's prices in Hong Kong or Antwerp.

Ask almost anyone you meet what they think about U.S. housing prices, and they will probably say, "They're too high!" The perception of high prices is, in reality, what counts. Of course, people often willingly pay what they consider to be high prices, *if* they can see a profit in it. If you're looking at a home which today costs $100,000, but which you firmly believe will be worth $110,000 in one year, you might overlook the "high" price. Sure, you'll be paying a lot, but you'll probably feel it's worth it in the end.

In a way, it's like the old pyramid games which became popular toward the end of the recent housing boom. John buys a home and sells it to Jane six months later for a $5,000 profit. After six months, Jane sells it to Harry for a $6,000 profit. After another six months, Harry sells it to Sally for a $7,000 profit.

Did Sally buy because she thought the value was there in the home? Probably not. She bought because she saw what happened to John, Jane and Harry, and she wanted her profit, too. Sally hoped to make a killing in price appreciation. Of course, the old pyramid game only works with more and more people joining in. Sally succeeds only if she can find someone else after six months who is willing to buy, giving her a big profit.

As a rule, however, pyramid games eventually collapse of their own weight, and something similar has happened in housing. Once it became clear that the anticipated appreciation wasn't going to happen—that you couldn't sell in six months for $5,000 or more profit—people asked themselves, "Why should I spend so much?" So Sally got stuck with the house. She could live in it and wait for time and inflation to catch up with the price she paid. Or she could sell it at a loss.

If we consider prices alone, then it might be fair to say that by 1981 we were seeing 1985 prices in real estate. The housing market has simply gone too far and too fast. During the late 1970s, when the U.S. dollar was losing value to inflation, all prices, including that of housing, rose dramatically. When people bailed out of dollars and into harder assets—from rare coins to antiques to gold and silver—the prices of these harder assets also increased.

Today, however, high interest rates have made investing in dollars (in money-market funds, T-bills, commercial paper, etc.) highly profitable, resulting in a drive away from hard assets. Rare coin prices, for example, have declined as much as 25 percent since their highs. Diamonds would have collapsed were it not for the DeBeers cartel withholding new rough from the market. Anyone who has followed the papers has seen the decline of gold and silver.

Real estate is no exception—the prices it shot up to were simply too high to be sustained. They weren't warranted by increased costs of construction. (Ten years ago, *land* costs were only about 15 percent of the value of a new home. Today they are closer to 40 percent, and land is not a "construction" cost.) The staggering price of housing is now helping to strangle the real estate market—it's just very hard today to find a sucker to pay more for your house than you did.

Financing

Some people have said that financing, more than anything else, is strangling real estate. They're probably right. Throughout 1981 and into 1982, interest rates were prohibitively high. To obtain a $100,000 mortgage at 17 percent interest, for example, required monthly payments of over $1,400 *before* taxes, insurance and utilities. Only about eight out of every 100 American families could afford to buy. And it's unlikely that the problem will soon go away.

Savings and loan associations, the major lenders for real estate, got caught flat-footed when interest rates soared. They were paying their depositors 15 percent and more while receiving an average of nine percent on their long-term mortgages. The S&L industry vowed never to let that unhappy situation occur again.

Today, nearly all mortgages are "adjustable," which means that interest charges will go down during periods of easy money, but rates will soar when money is tight. Today, when you buy a home, you don't really know what interest rate you're going to pay. The mortgage might say 10% interest, but if economic conditions change, it could be 15 percent by the end of a year!

Most families simply can't handle that kind of an increase. To get around it, some lenders have agreed to a monthly payment "cap" of, say, five percent, regardless of what happens to the interest rate. With a five percent "cap" on a $100 monthly payment, our payment couldn't go to more than $105 regardless of what the interest rate on our mortgage did.

In this case, however, the cure can be worse than the disease. If the interest-rate increase is higher than the cap allows, the excess interest money is added to our principal. This is called "negative amortization." Instead of paying off our mortgage, we owe more each year! It's interest on interest. (For a thorough explanation of the new mortgages, see *The New Mortgage Game*, Robert Irwin, McGraw-Hill, 1982.)

Today, when we buy we take on the lender as a partner. And this has important implications for profit. Why should we struggle to make outrageous payments on a home when, if it increases in value by the time we sell, we must share the profit with the lender in the form of interest added to our mortgage principal?

This situation with financing is causing many would-be buyers to reconsider renting as a viable alternative.

Tax Crises

Ask any broker what the big incentive is for buying instead of renting a home.

The answer is simple and obvious—when you rent you get no tax benefits, but when you buy, you can write off the taxes you pay to local government and the interest you pay on your mortgage. If you have a $100,000 mortgage at 17 percent, with $17,000 in interest payments plus an additional $3,000 in taxes, your tax deduction is $20,000. In the fifty percent tax bracket, you save $10,000 that would otherwise be paid in taxes.

WRITE-OFF

$20,000	interest and taxes paid during year deducted from federal taxes
× 50%	tax bracket
$10,000	tax savings

The home is, in fact, the only tax shelter for most middle-income Americans.

But there is a movement afoot to do away with both the interest write-off and the tax write-off on homes! Don't think it's impossible. Three times since Gerald Ford was president, major efforts have been made to abolish the deductions for home interest and for taxes. The latest occurred in early 1982. The Reagan Administration, faced with towering federal deficits of over $100 billion a year (caused in part by the massive tax cuts it engineered in 1981), looked for ways to increase tax revenues. One avenue considered was eliminating the interest and tax deductions for homes. The administration estimated that it could save over $30 billion in 1982 and over $80 billion by 1983.

As of this writing, the outcome of this latest effort has not been decided. Should it fail, however, people from the Treasury Department and other interest groups will continue to press for this "reform." Eventually, the deductions for interest and taxes on homes probably will be eliminated or at least limited.

When that happens, we can expect to see unparalleled foreclosures in community after community as prices collapse in the housing market. Home prices could fall by as much as a third when people discover what their housing costs are without the government tax subsidy. Rather than paying more taxes because they've lost the big home deduction they anticipated, many people will simply walk away from their homes. Selling your home in such a market would be like offering salt water to a swimmer in the Pacific.

Rent Control

In this book, we're considering the housing market not as a place for us to live in, but as a place for us to buy and rent. Rent is the key word. To make a profit here, we have to be able to rent our house for at least what our monthly payments are. In nearly all areas of the country, this has been impossible since at least 1978. Rents have not kept pace with mortgage costs and taxes. In California, for example, it is possible today in the Los Angeles area to buy a condominium unit for $80,000. This unit can be rented for perhaps $500 per month. But, the payments—including taxes, insurance and homeowner's fees—are about $1,000 per month. That's an imbalance of about half.

Yet, with the tax benefits (plus depreciation on investment real estate) and the knowledge that prices were going up, many investors sacrificed to meet the negative cash flow, hoping for that pot of gold at the end of the rainbow. Besides, they figured that they could always raise rents. The condo that rents for $500 today will rent for $600 a year from now. In two or three years, with luck, the monthly rent might even go high enough to meet the monthly mortgage, tax, and other expenses.

Except for rent control—another finger around the throat of the housing market. Hundreds of cities across the country, and most major ones, have some form of rent control in effect right now. It's easy to see why people want rent control. Many renters—the elderly, widows and widowers, and young couples—are the people least able to withstand rent increases. To protect them, well-meaning local governments have created rent controls. Most local governments fail to see, however, that by artificially keeping rents down, they make it unprofitable to build new units. And the building of new units—increasing the supply of rentable housing—is the only way rental prices stabilize.

Thus far, in most areas, rent control has only affected apartment buildings of more than four units. In some places, however, even single-family homes have come under rent control. And the writing is on the wall. As fewer homes are built (new housing construction in 1981 was off by more than 50 percent) and fewer investors buy homes, the pressure will be on to increase rents in houses and condominiums. Owners will find that competition for housing allows them to raise rents higher and higher, until tenants' complaints lead to rent control of even single-family housing.

Management

Management is the hidden expense in owning a house (or condo) as an investment. I've never seen a broker or an investor put down a figure for management costs of single-unit housing. It's always assumed that the investor will take care of it himself.

That's a big assumption, as anyone who has owned an investment home knows. Besides rent collection, mortgage and tax payments, and other accounting chores, there's the headache of repairs and maintenance. Water heaters tend to flood kitchens, garages or utility rooms at two in the morning. Roofs leak, plumbing goes bad, and heating fails; then there's repainting and fixing to do before new tenants are willing to move in.

Management of single units always has been troublesome. But, in the past the considerable profit made it worthwhile. In the future, however, with less profit to be made, management of single units looms as a much larger burden, particularly when compared with other types of real estate that are relatively management-free. As an investor, it comes down to a simple matter of saying "Who needs the headache?" In a bad market, management is another reason for not investing in single-unit property.

These, then, are the five fingers around the throat of single-family homes and condos: high prices, tough financing, potential loss of tax benefits, possible rent controls, and management headaches. They are significant concerns which are not going to go away. And they are solid reasons why I think all real estate investors should consider alternatives to the single-family home or condominium.

WHY HOUSING PRICES MIGHT BOOM

But, to be fair, it's important to recognize the reasons that prices for single-family houses or condos might again go up. As I see it, there is only one reason.

Demand

There is an incredible demand for housing here in the United States. In 1970, a government study estimated that at least 2.5 million new housing units would be needed each year until 1990 to keep up with the demand. (In 1981, less than 500,000 were built!) The housing industry could quadruple its production and still there would be a shortage of housing.

The demand comes from a variety of sources, the biggest of which is probably the *baby-boom generation*. It has been estimated that during the 1980s an additional ten million people (over and above the number in the 1970s) will marry, form families and seek homes. This group is putting an enormous demand on the already tight housing market, and its pressure is likely to last until the end of this decade.

Increased numbers of elderly citizens further increases the demand for housing. Modern advances in medicine have enabled more of us to live longer, which means that more housing is needed for the elderly. This is a particularly tough problem, because older Americans generally have low or fixed incomes. (See *The $125,000 Decision, The Older Americans Guide to Retirement Housing,* Robert Irwin, McGraw-Hill, 1982.)

Changes in lifestyle add to the demand for housing. Today, both spouses in a marriage tend to work, which makes it economically feasible to consider divorce. And increasing divorces mean that one unit will no longer adequately house the family.

Immigration also puts a demand on housing. In the last few years, we've absorbed refugees from Viet Nam, Russia, Haiti, and Cuba, in addition to the tens of thousands from Europe, the Middle East and South America who have opted to live in these United States.

This combination of baby-boom adults, the elderly, the divorced, and a massive influx of immigrants is causing an unprecedented demand for housing. This is reflected nation-wide in vacancy rates. In most cities, the rate is below five percent; but in the West and the Sunbelt, where many people are moving, it is often below two percent. The demand is simply using up available housing. While we don't yet have people living in the streets, we already have people doubling up—two families sharing the same house. This enormous demand for housing could potentially overwhelm all the reasons that the single-unit residential market might collapse. It could unlock the stranglehold that is depressing prices and could then force appreciation upward.

But will it?

Yes, I think so! But *only* in certain geographic areas of the country—including parts of Florida, Texas, California, Arizona, Washington, and Oregon—in general, the Sunbelt and the West. And the boom won't be equal throughout these areas. (In a later chapter, I'll have more specific things to say about the right places to buy.)

The point here is *not* that houses or condominiums are a bad investment. In selected areas, where enormous demand forces price appreciation, they will be a good investment. It's just that you can no longer buy *any* house *any*where in the country and expect the price to go up.

To be successful in the 1980s, the smart money is in diversification.

DIVERSIFICATION

You should grab the opportunity to invest in a single-family house or condominium, if your area is one of strong price appreciation. However, in most areas of the country today, the opportunities in single-family houses or condos are discouragingly small.

Yet, where the market in single-family homes or condos is strangling, at the same time and in the same place, commercial property may be booming! While houses are declining in price, the value of office space, small strip shopping centers, or retail stores may be jumping. The person who looks only to houses and condos in today's real estate market is wearing blinders, severely limiting the available opportunities.

The idea is to diversify your interests. Find out what type of real estate (beyond houses and condos) is booming in your area, and then see if you can get involved with it. In some cases, it may take no more money than that needed to buy a house! For example, on the East Coast—in New York, Maryland and several other areas—the conversion of apartment buildings to condominiums is flourishing. It's a real money-maker, as we'll see in chapter 6.

Diversifying means getting out of the single-family home or condo rut. It means looking at the broader horizons of investment real estate to find the special benefits that housing no longer enjoys.

Financing

While the reverse used to be true, well-priced investment property is now sometimes easier to finance than homes. Today, virtually the only mortgages available for homes are Adjustable Rate Mortgages of one sort or another, usually at staggeringly high interest rates. The reason is that tight money is forcing the savings and loan associations—the biggest suppliers of home-mortgage money—out of the field. On the other hand, money is available for investment real estate—at both fixed and adjustable rates—from a wide variety of sources that include venture capital, pensions funds, insurance companies, banks, and more.

Perhaps more important, when you buy a house *you* have to qualify by demonstrating you have enough income to make the payments. When you buy investment property, the *property* has to show sufficient income to make the payments. Normally, you need principally demonstrate good business and management ability.

That's not to say that investment-property financing is easy. It's not. But it is readily available, which isn't the case with homes today.

Management

In most cases, the homeowner personally manages the house. That means he's the one who gets the phone calls about broken toilets at two in the morning.

With investment property, there is often sufficient income to hire managers to handle this kind of work. Also, with the exception of apartment buildings, tenants are usually business people whose leases cover maintenance services (not to mention your taxes and insurance!). A twenty-unit office building is often more easily managed than two houses.

Capital

When you buy a house, in some instances you can't qualify for a new first mortgage if you're borrowing the money for the down payment. Typically, the money has to come out of your savings. When buying investment property, usually no one cares where the investment capital is coming from. You can borrow it with little concern about squashing the deal.

In addition, through the use of limited partnerships, it is often fairly easy to band together with relatives, friends and associates to raise sufficient capital to make the down payment on a large building—sometimes without investing a dime of your own!

Passive Investment

Numerous, small limited partnerships are available today where you can invest your money and the partnership will own, manage and eventually sell the property. You won't have any direct responsibilities for it. This can be either good or bad, depending on the property and the partnership, as we'll see in the chapter on raising capital. But, with a good partnership, it can be very profitable indeed.

Tax Benefits

The tax benefits for investment property are similar to those of owning an investment home (except for recapture, detailed in chapter four). But with investment property, you generally own a much *bigger* piece of real estate, which means that your tax benefits are often much greater than with a single home.

Opportunity

Everyone and their uncles are out looking for a great investment home to buy today. Remembering the price booms of the last decade, they blindly assume that the same conditions will continue to prevail. As we've seen, today's pressures are unlikely to allow this.

Very few investors are out looking for small- to medium-sized investment property, and most of the investors out there have been in the field for years. There's very little new blood. Compared to investment houses, the competition simply isn't there. The biggest problem for new investors is having less available capital, which means they must settle for the smaller investments in the beginning—the ones the big boys have passed over—until they get to be the big boys themselves.

Investment real estate is the future. In this book, we'll cover many of the opportunities available out there today. Before we do, however, it's necessary to get a good fix on the difference between buying homes and buying other property. In the next three chapters, we'll concentrate on evaluation, taxation and raising capital for investment real estate.

Chapter Three

HOW TO EVALUATE INCOME PROPERTY

Because real estate involves big bucks, you'd think that people would evaluate investments with great care. Some of us do. Others, however, blinded by the flash of big profits, jump right in without first testing the water. Nobody wants to buy a "pig in a poke" or throw their money away on a worthless investment. So, the first question with any investment is how much is it really worth?

Say you find a terrific office building or small shopping center, and the seller tells you there's a lot of profit to be made. It might be a good deal, but how do you know? How do you know what price you must pay to break even, or to make a profit? How much cash should you put down? How heavy should the leveraging be? Is the seller's price too high, or is it a real bargain? Does the property make economic sense? Is it a good investment? In this chapter we'll discover how to quickly and easily determine the true value of investment real estate.

For the purposes of this chapter, think of yourself as a "wheeler and dealer" in real estate—a successful investor with lots of money in your pocket. You're ready to move into more profitable properties, but you're also wary. You know that sellers exaggerate the value of property, and you certainly don't want to get cheated. How do you know what to pay for a piece of income property?

EVALUATING NON-INCOME-PRODUCING PROPERTY

An income-producing property is not just a bigger house than you now own. It's a different kind of animal that requires different evaluation. But before we see how it's different, we first must know how it's similar. Let's consider how single-family housing is evaluated.

Jane has a house that she wants to sell. How does she know its value? First, she calls a few brokers and selects one who sounds intelligent and honest. Don, our broker, measures Jane's house up and down and all around, then notes all the "extras"—upgraded carpeting, air conditioning, trash compactor, good paint, spa in the back yard, and so on. Then he spreads a computer printout across her dining room table showing "comparables"—past sales of similar homes—and says that the comparable sheet will show what price she can get. Don points out that Jane's home is in the Green Valley tract of homes built about seven years earlier, and that her four-bedroom, two-bath model was known as plan A-7. The computer has called up four sales of Green Valley A-7 homes in the past six months, which sold in a range from $110,000 to $115,000. The computer also notes that the most expensive home had a spa, and that the least expensive one needed new carpeting. Then Don does a worksheet—allowing for all the extras in Jane's home, but depreciating them for their age—and comes up with a figure of $114,000. "That's what your house is worth on the market today," he says.

Don's method of evaluation was basically one of comparing prices. (Other methods, such as considering the replacement cost of the home and the value of the lot, could have been used.) While earlier prices realized did not guarantee that any particular price would produce a sale, Don felt they were a good indicator when condition of the property and extra features were added in. Why? Using comparables is a shorthand method of determining *supply and demand* (which for our purposes also will include popularity of a particular home design and location).

In economics, we learn that price is what brings supply and demand together. Those with houses must price them in such a way that buyers will find the cost attractive. Each year, there are probably in excess of four million home sales across the country, tens of thousands in some cities, and hundreds in individual communities. Overall, it is supply and demand that, in a rough way, sorts out all the houses and buyers in a hierarchy of prices.

That's how prices are generally determined for non-income property. Now, let's consider income property.

EVALUATING INCOME-PRODUCING PROPERTY

In general, people buy homes to live in. The profit motive certainly may be there, but most home buyers are looking first for shelter. Not so with income-producing property. Here the first priority is making money, and in most cases, it is the only motive in making a purchase. Therefore, when calculating price, there must be a method of evaluating the profit to be made by investing in a particular piece of real estate, as compared to the potential profit in investing a similar amount of money elsewhere.

After selling her home, Jane had $50,000 in cash she wanted to invest, and she considered a variety of investments from real estate to gold coins. How was she to evaluate and compare each of them? Here are some of the considerations which should be made:

- How safe is the investment?
- What is the yield (return) on money invested?
- Is it liquid?
- Will it appreciate in value?
- Are there tax benefits or drawbacks?
- What about management headaches?
- Can the investment be used as collateral for financing?

No one investment will provide positive answers to all these questions. Stocks, for example, are highly liquid, relatively safe, and offer no management headaches. But, they haven't shown much appreciation in value, and there are few tax benefits, if any. Similarly, money-market mutual funds tend to be safe and liquid, with a good yield and no management headaches, but their *appreciation* is virtually nil. Gold tends to be volatile and unsafe, with no yield, tax benefits, or management headaches. It can be used as collateral for financing in certain cases. But, if your timing is right, it can appreciate enormously in value in just a short time.

Investment real estate, on the other hand, offers a benefit package which most investors find desirable. Investment real estate is relatively safe—it can offer a strong yield, show great appreciation, provide tax benefits, and be used as collateral for financing. The two greatest drawbacks are that the money invested is usually illiquid (you can't get it out in the short term), and there can be management headaches, although these can be minimized by the kind of real estate that is purchased.

After considering all these, Jane opted for an investment real estate purchase.

We've seen how to evaluate one type of an investment from another. Now, how do we evaluate investment real estate—one piece from another?

The Income Approach

Jane is basically concerned with two things: the return *on* her money and the return *of* her money. In real estate, the return of money is presumed to come about upon sale of the property. Therefore, in most cases, we don't have to be concerned directly with the return of our money. We know it's going to be invested in the property for a long time and we'll get it back when we sell.

We are concerned with the return *on* our money, which takes two forms in real estate. The first is the *annual return* during our time of ownership. The second is the *return we can expect from appreciation at the time we sell.*

Let's first consider the return during our term of ownership, which is calculated in a manner similar to that for any business—it is the difference between income and expenses.

Jane found an office building that she liked and wanted to buy. The "net income" from rentals, after deducting for such expenses as maintenance, insurance, and vacancies, came to $25,000 a year. (As we'll see in Chapter 10, tenants are often responsible for taxes, insurance and maintenance in "net leases," but for now we'll assume that these costs are Jane's.) The owner was asking $200,000 for the building. How was Jane to know if it was worth the money?

The first method Jane used to determine the true price was to find the ratio of the building's income to its cost and then to compare it with the yield from other investments. This very old method—called "capitalizing the net income"—isn't all that helpful today, when high-interest-rate mortgages play such a big role in income property. But, it is a good place to start and it helps us to understand other means of evaluation.

When Jane compared the income to the asking price, she did it very simply:

$$\frac{25,000}{200,000} = 1/8 \text{ or } 12.5\%$$

The net income (or "cap rate") was sufficient to provide a return of 12.5% on the asking price. Jane could now compare this figure with her yield from stocks, bonds, money-market funds, T-bills, or other investments. (If she did, she'd quickly find that 12.5 percent is a good but not great return.) She could also use it as a comparison tool to see whether her building was more or less competitively priced. Of course, Jane isn't going to invest $200,000 (should she pay full asking price). She only has $50,000. How is the equation affected when Jane has to *borrow* the rest to make the purchase?

Adding Mortgage Debt to the Cap Rate

In the real world, people rarely pay *cash* for real estate. Therefore, what's the point of knowing the income-to-price ratio when that income is going to be significantly reduced by our mortgage payments? Only by taking debt into account, can we get a true picture of our return and see whether the building is worth buying for $200,000.

There are many methods of doing this. We'll consider three:

Considering Investment Equity Only

This approach eliminates the mortgage element to concentrate only on the equity the investor will be putting into the property.

Jane is going to get a new mortgage for $150,000 on the property. The seller has agreed to give Jane that mortgage himself and will carry it for 30 years at a reduced interest rate of 14 percent. The annual mortgage payments come to $21,312.

net income	$25,000
mortgage payment	$21,312
annual cash flow	$ 3,688

Subtracting the mortgage payment from the net income, Jane finds she will have a net cash flow of $3,688. This figure is now used to give her a return on her investment.

$$\frac{3,688}{50,000} = 7.4\%$$

By this method, Jane can expect an unimpressive 7.4% return on her investment. She may feel, however, that she should be getting at least 10% on her money. If that's the case, she can quickly determine the correct price to pay for the property:

Three thousand six hundred eighty-eight dollars divided by 10 percent = $36,880. To get her desired 10 percent return on her equity, the most money Jane can put into the property is $36,880.

mortgage	$ 150,000
cash down	$− 36,880
	$ 186,880 selling price

According to this method, Jane should offer no more than $186,880.

(In the next chapter, on tax benefits, we'll see why the $3,688 isn't really the true yield on the property and why the seller probably wouldn't accept $187,000. But for now, let's just keep this method in the back of our minds.)

Weighted Rate

Another method Jane might use is the weighted rate, which is found by combining the return on her invested equity with the return expected from mortgages and comparing the total with her net income. Although the seller is offering a 14 percent rate on a 75 percent of value loan, the current rate in the area is 15 percent on an 80 percent mortgage.

.15 × .80 = .12   current mortgage rate and amount
.10 × .20 = .02   return Jane would like and her amount
                                of investment
                 .14   weighted rate

The return on this property should be 14 percent when anticipated mortgage return and equity return are combined, and we know that the net income is $25,000. By dividing $25,000 by 14 percent, we find that the appropriate value of the property is $178,571.

$$
\begin{array}{r}
\$25,000 \\
\div \quad 14\% \\
\hline
\$178,571
\end{array}
$$

Thus, factoring in the going rate for area mortgages, we learn that the property actually should be worth even less than we found by the investment-equity method.

	value
investment-equity method	$ 186,880
weighted rate	$−178,571
difference	$ 8,309

It could be said that the below-market interest rate offered by the owner (under the investment-equity method) has made the property worth a little over $8,000 more to us. Nevertheless, it is doubtful the owner would sell for $178,500.

What's wrong here? We've used two approaches that take debt into account, and we've come up with two answers, both considerably below the asking price. Is the seller wrong or are we? How do we reconcile all this?

One way is to look at an approach that considers debt from a different viewpoint. This method analyzes the cash flow.

Cash-Flow Analysis

Considering the cash flow coming back to us is similar to using the investment-equity method, but with a twist.

You'll recall that under the investment-equity method, we calculated that there would be $3,688 in positive cash flow by subtracting mortgage payments from net income. Dividing the cash flow by the down payment, we found that the return was a lowly 7.4 percent, at which Jane turned up her nose. Jane's reasoning was that the *only* return on her money was going to come from her positive cash flow. In reality, however, that's not the case. In addition, there is also the return of principal on the mortgage, which is of great significance in older mortgages.

In a new mortgage, virtually the entire monthly payment goes to pay the interest. But as the mortgage ages, more and more of the monthly payment goes to pay the principal. By the time a 30-year mortgage is 20 years old, most of each payment goes toward principal. If Jane were buying a building with an old mortgage, this return of principal would add to the yield she is getting on the building.

Additionally, there are tax benefits derived primarily from depreciation. As we'll see in the next chapter, on taxation, if Jane is in a high tax bracket, the tax benefits on her building can be higher than her cash flow!

Finally, there is the matter of appreciation. When she sells the building, Jane will not only get back all *of* her money, she will probably realize a considerable increase due to price appreciation. This, too, can be considered a return *on* her money. Many investors, in fact, look at cash flow as only a small part of the "yield" on their investment. Others look upon cash flow as "gravy"—they don't consider it to be *any* part of the yield.

Therefore, assuming we can find properties requiring nearly equal cash investments and yielding nearly equal profits at sales time, one way to consider value is to compare their cash flow. The building with the largest cash flow could be the best buy. Also, many investors "require" a certain cash flow, as an assurance of the safety of their investment and as a return on capital. This required rate typically varies between 5 and 9 percent. Let's assume that it's 7 percent. How does the price of Jane's building hold up now?

$ 3,688	cash flow
÷ .07	cash-flow rate desired
$ 52,686	cash which can be invested
$150,000	first mortgage
$202,686	value

By this method, the building is worth roughly what the seller is asking.

Putting It All Together

We've considered four distinct methods of evaluating Jane's investment, and we've come up with four different values. Which one should we use? It's my belief that, of the four methods considered—capping net income, considering investment equity only, weighted rate, and cash-flow analysis—cash-flow analysis works best in today's market. The reason is that the first three simply do not take appreciation into account.

Accounting for Appreciation

Investment property appreciates rapidly, and sellers know that the buyer's return will come mainly from future appreciation. So, to get some of that appreciation for themselves, sellers jack up the price beyond what is justified by most of the income-evaluation methods we've just described.

For example, let's say that by most income approaches Jane's property is currently worth $180,000, and let's further assume that it appreciates at the rate of 5 percent a year. What's it going to be worth in five years?

year	initial price		180,000
1	5%	appreciation	189,000
2	5%	"	198,450
3	5%	"	208,372
4	5%	"	218,791
5	5%	"	229,730

After five years, the property will have appreciated by roughly $50,000. This is the appreciation return that Jane can anticipate if she buys at $180,000, independent of the positive cash flow and substantial tax benefits we'll cover in the next chapter.

Most sellers want part of that future value today. So, instead of asking $180,000 which the income warrants, they might ask for $200,000. This is the way the real estate investment market operates today. So, we have to take appreciation into account to find the appropriate value of the investment.

Finding a method that accounts for future value can be difficult. We could, of course, simply project a 5 percent appreciation five years into the future. But we can't know with certainty what the actual appreciation will be—it could be 5 percent or any other amount. Determining future appreciation is tantamount to gambling on the horses or playing roulette. It's simply not possible to do with any assurance of accuracy.

How, then, is investment property evaluated for future profit?

The answer is that a method is used which is similar in principle to that used in evaluating homes—a comparison method.

GROSS INCOME MULTIPLIER (GIM)

The "gross income multiplier" is the most frequently used method for evaluating income property. It has its advocates as well as its detractors. Its proponents usually point out that the method quickly gives a reasonably accurate estimation of future value. Its detractors point out that, at best, it approximates value, and, at worst, it's grossly inefficient in accounting for major differences between investment properties. My own feeling is that the GIM is an invaluable tool which is extraordinarily simple to use and understand. When used with other tools, it can develop a highly accurate means of determining investment-property value.

What is the gross income multiplier?

It is a number, usually between seven and fourteen, which we multiply by the *gross* annual income from a piece of property. (Larger multipliers are used in conjunction with monthly income.) The property that Jane is considering, for example, had a gross income of about $25,000 a year. If the multiplier were eight, we would multiply the gross income by that figure.

$$
\begin{array}{r}
\$\ 25,000 \\
\times \qquad 8 \\
\hline
\$200,000
\end{array}
$$

According to this method, the value of the property (the price) should be about $200,000. But is it really that simple? Where did the number come from, and is it an accurate value? Does it apply to all kinds of real estate investments? Obviously, our example here is far too simplified. Let's expand it by first examining where the gross income multiplier comes from.

Jane is planning to buy an apartment building and wants to know its value. She finds this by comparing the values of other apartment buildings that have sold recently. The process is similar to comparing other home sales to find the value of her home.

There is, however, a big difference. When speaking of home sales, we mentioned that people buy homes principally to use as shelter, and that when they buy investment property, their principal desire is to make money. In comparing homes, we simply looked at prices. But, when we compare income properties, we have to add in the return that is received from rental each year. While price was our only concern in houses, prices *and* income concern us in investment property.

Determining the Multiplier

Price and income combine to form the gross income multiplier. Here's how. Jane looked over records of recent sales, trying to find buildings of comparable location, size, income-to-expense ratios, services (such as furnished or not), and so on. Then she looked at their income in relation to their price and discovered the following:

	Annual Income	Sales Price
Building A	$ 10,000	$ 80,000
Building B	150,000	1,200,000
Building C	2,000	16,000
Building D	30,000	240,000
Building E	50,000	400,000

Each of the buildings had a different annual income and a different sales price. But, looking more closely, we see something which all the units have in common. When their sales price is divided by their annual income, the resulting number is eight for all five buildings. This tells Jane that apartment buildings are selling for about eight times their gross income. The GIM, therefore, is eight, which Jane used to determine the $200,000 value on the apartment building she was considering.

Problems with the Multiplier

In the real world, of course, things usually aren't quite this tidy. Rarely will all the comparables come in at the same multiplier. While some may be eight, others may be ten, six, or seven. Therefore, the multiplier used will have to be a composite.

Additionally, the gross income multiplier alone tells us little about individual apartment buildings. Using the same multiplier, we would come up with identical prices for two buildings which had identical gross incomes. One building, however, might have a positive cash flow and the other a negative one. The cash flow may be a significant factor in our evaluation of the building, which the GIM alone wouldn't tell us.

To quickly find the cash flow and direction, two formulas are commonly used by investors in conjunction with the GIM.

Debt Ratio

The debt ratio is simply the percentage of the gross income that goes to paying off the debt or mortgage on a building. If the income is $10,000 a year and the mortgage payments are $7,000, we know that the debt ratio is 70 percent:

$$\frac{\$\ 7,000}{\$10,000} = 7/10 \text{ or } 70\%$$

Expense Ratio

On the other hand, if expenses, with the exception of mortgage and other payments (including taxes, maintenance and repairs), are compared with the income, we get the expense ratio.

If the expenses on this property are $5,000 a year (exclusive of mortgage etc.), then the expense ratio is 50 percent.

$$\frac{\$\ 5,000}{\$10,000} = 5/10 \text{ or } 50\%$$

The combined debt and expense ratios on this investment property are 120%. What does that mean? Put simply, it means that we need 120% of income to meet all costs, or $12,000 in this case. Since income is $10,000, we'll need $2,000 out of pocket just to keep the property solvent. *Combined ratios over 100% mean negative cash flow. Below 100% we have positive cash flow.*

Having estimated the property value with the GIM, an investor then uses the debt and expense ratios to learn how much the building will return or cost, so he can adjust the price accordingly. A building with positive cash flow is surely worth more than one with negative cash flow.

Changing Multipliers

As we've seen, the relationship between the income of investment property and the price of past sales gives us a GIM to use in determining current value. But, let's go back one generation of sales. How were the prices we used in our earlier examples determined? How did the buyers and sellers of building D, for example, arrive at their gross income multiplier? The obvious answer is that they compared sales even further in the past.

By this reasoning, we could go ever backward to previous sales to justify current prices. Also, by this reasoning, it's hard to see how the multiplier could ever be anything but eight. In actual practice, however, while eight, seven and six were commonly found multipliers in the mid-1970s, by the 1980s, multipliers from 10 to 14 became common. But, how can the multipliers have changed so radically, if they are based on previous prices?

Multiplier Inflation

The answer is the one Jane found when she wanted to sell her house. You'll recall that from comparables between $110,000 and $115,000, the broker arrived at a price for Jane's home of $114,000. But Jane felt that real estate prices would be going up, and she wanted more. Unfortunately, they weren't, and she had to settle for less.

The same thing happens with investment property. When sellers realize that demand is strong, they ask a higher price than past multipliers would indicate. The income from the property remains the same, yet the price rises. The result is an increase in the GIM. Consider:

Income	Old Price	Old GIM	New Price	New GIM
$10,000	$80,000	8	$120,000	12

An increased demand for real estate results in a multiplier inflation. But, why has demand increased for investment property? Because people anticipate that the price of real estate which has appreciated in the past will continue to do so. Anticipating future growth, investors *compete* with one another for investment property, and the competition results in increased demand and higher multipliers. (The reverse is also true—reduced demand means lower multipliers.) To put it another way, increased gross income multipliers allow sellers to get some of that *future profit today*.

To see this more clearly, let's go back to our building A with a gross income of $10,000. When the multiplier was eight, the price was $80,000. If we assume the mortgage is 80 percent of price, or $64,000, then the annual payments are about $9,000, and the debt ratio is 90%. On the other hand, with a GIM of 12, the price of the same property is now $120,000. Assuming the same 80% mortgage, or $96,000, the annual mortgage payments are now approximately $13,600, and the debt ratio is 136%. With a debt ratio of 136 percent, the negative cash flow is going to be horrendous. Why would anyone pay $120,000 for such a piece of property? Why would an investor stand for a gross income multiplier of 12?

The Multiplier and Future Value

The reason (besides the tax advantages) is the *future value* of the property. Such investors bank on a high appreciation rate, feeling that the property they bought with a GIM of 12 will be resold at a huge profit in a few years. They are counting on increasing rental income, so that the annual income grows ever higher, and future income eventually justifies today's price.

The gross income multiplier, therefore, measures the future value of property in an indirect way. It reflects what both buyer and seller think the property will be worth in the future, and it allows the present price to take that future value into consideration.

The Multiplier and Negative Cash Flow

The unfortunate result of multiplier inflation (as sellers try to cash in on tomorrow's prices) is that investment property is put into negative-cash-flow situations. This should be fairly obvious. When a property is just breaking even at a multiplier of 8, increasing that multiplier to 14 or higher (and thereby increasing the price) means that the same cash flow has to handle more equity and, perhaps, more financing. This results in a negative cash flow, or in the investor using out-of-pocket money to handle the building.

In today's market in many parts of the country, houses, condos and apartment buildings have negative cash flow as the rule. Very few such properties offer the chance to break even. So, it is usually necessary for the buyer to raise 25–50 percent of the income required to cover expenses, out of pocket! Of course, investors have plunged into such deals banking on future appreciation and counting on tax advantages, but theirs may be a pipe dream in our weak economy. It is possible to buy other types of investment property without big negatives. Some office buildings, for example, still offer economically sound investment possibilities, and another reason for choosing investment real estate over homes (and condos).

By the multiplier method, we've seen that the value of Jane's prospective purchase is probably very close to the $200,000 asking price. The final question, however, is: "Should she pay it?"

Here we've evaluated the property using the property alone, but property is never bought or sold in a vacuum. When a buyer purchases property, that buyer has certain tax liabilities, and the benefits the property offers can affect those liabilities. Tax benefits, therefore, are the final consideration we must make in evaluating investment real estate.

Chapter Four

TAX BENEFITS
OF INCOME PROPERTY

"People don't buy income property to make money—they buy it to lose money!"

If you've heard that saying during the past decade, it's probably because the tax-shelter advantages of income property have sometimes overshadowed the economic benefits. Many investors have bought mainly to get a write-off, which is both good and bad. It's good in the sense that so many tax benefits are available from income real estate. But it's bad in that some investors have locked themselves into terrible purchases by wearing "tax-shelter" blinders. Hoping for a tax shelter, they bought property that had no chance of being a success.

In this chapter, we'll examine income property from the viewpoint of determining both its economic value and its tax benefits. It's important to remember that any piece of real estate must make good economic sense—it must be capable of showing a profit—before we consider the tax advantages.

(*Note:* The reader should be aware that the purpose of this chapter is not to give tax advice, but to explain how tax benefits in real estate contribute to property evaluation. For tax or legal advice on any piece of property or transaction, you should see your own accountant/CPA or attorney.)

STARTING TO DETERMINE THE TAX CONSEQUENCES

John has found an office building he wants to buy, which costs $200,000 and produces an income of $20,000 a year. Using the evaluative techniques from the previous chapter, John has determined that, given the current market conditions, the building is worth about $150,000, and the land about $50,000. He isn't interested in buying the building as a hobby; he wants to make money on it. "There has to be a profit sometime—each month, at the end of the year, or when I sell—but sometime!"

An obvious statement? Perhaps, but it's astonishing how many investors forget to make it. Instead, they just plunge into real estate, figuring that someday their profit will show up. They never bother to determine if there really ever will be a profit.

But not John. He was alert and determined to get a true evaluation of his prospective office-building purchase. Since he was in the 50 percent tax bracket, John wanted to know what tax benefits the building could offer him.

Depreciation

A simple concept in calculating taxes is that your gain (profit) is usually taxable. On the other hand, a loss is normally deductible. John knows that many pieces of real estate can show a substantial loss, on paper, once depreciation is calculated.

Depreciation is the gradual loss in value of a building for any cause. (For our purposes, the land does not lose value and cannot be depreciated.) An office building might last 30 to 40 years, but because of physical deterioration, change in neighborhood, obsolescence, or any other cause, it might no longer be able to produce income. No tenant would want to rent it.

At that point the building has lost value. An investor who originally bought it for, say, $150,000, would find that his investment had turned to zero. Instead of waiting until the property becomes worthless to write off an asset, however, the government allows investors to capitalize this loss over the years of ownership. They can take a little bit of the loss each year.

How can John predict whether or not the building he buys will still be producing rents ten years from now? Or twenty? Or fifty? What is the useful life of an office building? In the past, the useful life was arguable. Investors, hoping for bigger write-offs of depreciation each year, argued for a short useful life, while the government, wanting the most tax dollars they could get, argued for a longer life. In general, useful lives of 25 to 40 years were accepted.

The 1981 Economic Recovery Tax Act (ERTA) changed all that. The term now is set for all real estate at 15 years (although longer useful lives may be elected), which means that John may depreciate his property over a 15-year period. But, how does that relate to showing a loss on paper and, ultimately, to giving John a tax benefit? It all comes down to an income and expense sheet. Owning a piece of income property is like owning any other business. There are revenues received and costs which must be paid. Here's a typical income/expense sheet for an office building *before* depreciation is considered:

Income	
rent	$19,500
other (candy machines)	+ 500
	$20,000

Expenses	
taxes	$ 5,000
insurance	1,000
maintenance	1,000
interest portion of mortgage payment*	+ 12,000
	$19,000

INCOME	$20,000
EXPENSES	19,000
PROFIT	$ 1,000

*(*Note:* The principal part of the mortgage payment is really a return of debt and can't be considered an expense, even though it is part of the monthly payment.)

On the surface, it would appear that the office building turns a profit of $1,000 a year, but we haven't yet considered depreciation. Since depreciation is almost always taken into account, we speak of the difference between income and expenses before depreciation as "cash flow" rather than as "profit." In this case, the cash flow is positive—the building is returning money to the owner.

Now, let's consider depreciation. It is an expense item just like taxes or mortgage interest. In calculating depreciation, John has a couple of options.

First, on the building value of $150,000, John can simply take equal amounts of depreciation for each of the 15 years allowable (no salvage value is required under ERTA).

$$\begin{array}{r} \$150,000 \\ \div \quad 15 \text{ years} \\ \hline \$\ 10,000 \text{ per year} \end{array}$$

Under this method, John could deduct $10,000 a year for fifteen years as an operating expense for depreciation.

Accelerated Depreciation

But John could use the accelerated method of depreciation. With this method, a large portion of the depreciation is taken in the early years and a smaller one later on. The most popular method of calculating accelerated depreciation is the declining balance method. The current allowable rate is 175 percent of straight-line depreciation.

Multiplying the straight-line method by 175%, or 1.75, we get

$$\begin{array}{r} \$10,000 \\ \times \quad 1.75 \\ \hline \$17,500 \end{array}$$

Now, in the first year, John can take a deduction of $17,500 instead of one for $10,000. Note two important items here: first, the second year's depreciation under the declining balance method will be much less, because the depreciation already taken must be deducted from the value of the building.

$150,000	value
17,500	less depreciation already taken
$132,500	remaining value
÷ 15	years (straight-line method)
$ 8,833	straight-line depreciation at year two
× 175%	rate
$ 15,458	second year's depreciation

With this method, the balance to be depreciated declines enough in about six years that a switch to the straight-line method becomes advisable. (At year 15, the property will have zero value—$150,000 having been depreciated by either method.)

Secondly, it is important to be aware of the tax ramifications upon sale, if the accelerated method is used for other than residential income property. We'll cover this in a few moments.

Let's see what happens when the deduction for depreciation is now combined with other expenses:

USING STRAIGHT-LINE

INCOME			$20,000
EXPENSES	taxes, maintenance and interest	$19,000	
	depreciation	10,000	
	total expenses	$29,000	29,000
LOSS			$ (9,000)

USING ACCELERATED

INCOME			$20,000
EXPENSES	taxes, maintenance and interest	$19,000	
	depreciation	17,500	
	total expenses	$36,500	36,500
LOSS			$(16,500)

Depending on the method chosen, John can now show a loss on the office building of either $9,000 or $16,500. Keep in mind that this loss is basically "on paper." It does not take cash flow into account, which remains at $1,000 positive. So, John can show a tax loss at the same time that he's getting $1,000 in cash out of the property. But what is the tax loss actually worth to John as a write-off? The tax loss on the office building would be combined with his other income. Here's how it works out in terms of tax dollars saved, for the 50% and 30% tax brackets:

50% TAX BRACKET

STRAIGHT-LINE		ACCELERATED
$(9,000)	loss	$(16,500)
× 50%	tax bracket	× 50%
$ 4,500	tax savings	$ 8,250

30% TAX BRACKET

$(9,000)	loss	$(16,500)
× 30%	tax bracket	× 30%
$ 2,700	tax savings	$ 4,950

Depending on his tax bracket and the method of depreciation chosen, John can realize tax savings of as low as $2,700 or as high as $8,250. (Of course, we've assumed that John's tax bracket remained constant. The inclusion of the write-off might actually lower his bracket, which would then reduce the amount of tax savings. Also, savings would be different for different tax brackets.)

Since John was in the 50 percent bracket, he was looking at savings of either $4,500 or $8,250.

Obviously, John will consider this tax benefit when he makes a decision on whether or not to buy. But, before we see how, let me explain why we're giving John the option of approximately $4,500 or $8,000 in savings? Doesn't it make sense to opt for the higher amount?

INCOME DEFERRAL

This is a critical point in our understanding of how taxation affects real estate (and, in truth, all investments).

The money that John saves is not "tax-free." "Tax-free" refers to certain specific kinds of tax shelters, such as an "all-savers" certificate. There is no tax to pay on it.

But money saved from depreciation is *not* tax-free—it is only tax "deferred." That means that the taxes you save this year will have to be paid (most likely) in some future year, and the rate at which you must pay them is directly affected by the method of depreciation elected.

Here's how it works:

Capital Gains and the Straight-Line Method

If John chose the straight-line method and sold after two years, here's what his taxable gain would look like. We have now included the $50,000 land value in the $200,000 original value.

original value or basis	$200,000
2 years of straight-line depreciation	
($10,000 + $10,000)	20,000
new basis	$180,000

Depreciation taken lowers the basis (or value for tax purposes) of the property. If John sold two years later for just what he paid (not considering closing costs, improvements and other factors which influence basis and sales price), he would show a gain.

sales price	$200,000
less basis	180,000
gain	$ 20,000

If John sold for just what he paid and made no profit on the building, he'd still show a gain because of the way depreciation lowered his basis. (If he sold for more than what he paid, his gain would presumably be higher.) However, because he had held for over one year (and assuming he was not a "dealer" in real estate), he would qualify for capital-gains treatment. The maximum rate is currently 20 percent for someone in the 50 percent tax bracket.

$$\begin{array}{ll} \$20,000 & \text{gain} \\ \underline{\times \quad 20\%} & \text{maximum capital-gains rate} \\ \$\ 4,000 & \text{tax} \end{array}$$

Using the straight-line method, John wrote off $4,500 in taxes *per year* during two years of ownership, for a total of $9,000 in tax savings (see page 34).

However, at sale time, he must now pay the taxes that were deferred, although at the lower capital-gains tax rate.

$$\begin{array}{ll} \$9,000 & \text{tax savings (50\% rate) over two years} \\ \underline{-\ 4,000} & \text{taxes at time of sale (capital-gains 20\% rate)} \\ \$5,000 & \text{actual tax-dollar savings} \end{array}$$

If that seems complicated, I suggest that you reread the last few pages, which discuss the tax benefits of real estate. Too often, promoters and casual investors will forget that depreciation-caused tax savings are in reality *tax-deferred* dollars. They are not tax-free. The government still has to be paid.

The benefit here, of course, is that by deferring to the future, John moves money out of his ordinary tax rate of 50 percent into the more favorable capital-gains rate of 20 percent.

(Capital gain is figured in this manner. Sixty percent of the gain is excluded, and the remaining 40 percent is added to ordinary income. Forty percent times a 50 percent bracket yields a real tax rate of 20 percent.)

Recapture and the Accelerated Method

On the other hand, John might elect to use the accelerated method. As we described, here's his write-off for the first two years:

year one	$16,500
year two	+14,458
total write-off	$30,958
tax bracket	× 50%
savings	$15,479

Using the accelerated method during two years of ownership, John would have been able to save $15,479 in money
otherwise spent on taxes.

However, at the time of sale, there are *no capital gains allowed
on nonresidential income property if any accelerated depreciation was
taken*. He would have to pay taxes at the ordinary rate *on the
entire gain*. Here's his taxable gain.

Original value	$200,000
less depreciation taken	− 32,958
adjusted basis	$167,042
sales price	$200,000
less adjusted basis	167,042
gain	$ 32,958
tax bracket	× 50%
tax due	$ 16,479!

Because all of the depreciation was recaptured at ordinary
income tax-bracket rates, John ends up with no actual tax-
dollar savings at the end of two years. In fact, he ends up
paying additional taxes because of the $2,000 cash flow he
received.

Taxes upon sale because of recapture	$16,479
Tax savings during two years	
because of depreciation	−15,479
Additional tax after two years	$ 1,000!

What, then, is the possible advantage of taking accelerated
depreciation? With straight-line at least John would save $5,000
in taxes. With accelerated, he would save nothing and end up
paying taxes on the positive cash flow at a 50% rate.

It would make sense *if* John anticipated being in a *lower* tax bracket when he sold than he is now. If he is currently in the 50 percent tax bracket, but anticipates being in the 20 percent tax bracket when he sells, then the accelerated method might make sense.

(*Note:* Through the use of an installment sale, John might take only small parts of that gain over each of several years, thus keeping his tax bracket low. Or, through the use of a tax-deferred exchange, he might continue to roll the property over into new ones, and so continue deferring the tax into the future.)

Because John was involved in an office building, however, he could not combine the accelerated depreciation with the benefits of a capital-gains rate. *Nonresidential* property has full recapture.

Residential Property Recapture

If, however, John had bought an apartment building, a rental house, or a condominium, it would be a different story. *For residential property*, recapture is limited to only that portion of accelerated depreciation that exceeds straight-line. That may sound like a mouthful, but it's really quite simple.

Let's assume that John's office building is an apartment house. Here's what the figures would be for straight-line and accelerated after two years.

accelerated depreciation	$32,958
straight-line	− 20,000
difference	$12,958

If it were residential property, the $20,000 portion (or straight-line) would be eligible for capital-gains treatment. The difference between straight-line and accelerated, or $12,958, would be recaptured at ordinary income rates (50 percent in John's case).

There's an interesting side to this. If John were to own *residential* property and take the accelerated method, there would be no recapture at all after 15 years. The reason is that by year 15, or when the property is fully depreciated, *both* straight-line and accelerated equal zero. Since there is no excess of one over the other, there can be no recapture.

But, John wasn't buying residential property—he was buying an office building. Consequently, he wanted the eventual tax break offered by converting ordinary income into capital gains (figuring he'd continue to be in the 50 percent tax bracket). So he opted for the straight-line method.

Now, we have finally determined what depreciation method John will take (straight-line) and what his annual loss on the building will be because of it ($9,000 write-off = $4,500 tax savings in 50% bracket). How do these calculations help John decide whether or not to buy the building?

CALCULATING AFTER-TAX YIELD

You'll recall that income is the major way by which investment property is evaluated. The tax shelter created in John's office building produces income. We must now consider the total income the property will produce and weigh this against the investment.

First, let's try an income-capitalization approach. We said the office building produced a gross income of $20,000 and a net income of $13,000 after expenses, not including mortgage or depreciation. Let's add that net-income figure of $13,000 to the $4,500 in cash savings that John will get from tax benefits.

$$
\begin{array}{ll}
\$13,000 & \text{net income} \\
\underline{4,500} & \text{tax savings} \\
\$17,500 & \text{after-tax net income}
\end{array}
$$

Now we can compare this after-tax net income with the proposed sales price to get our new cap rate:

$$
\frac{\$\ 17,500}{\$200,000} \quad \begin{array}{l} \text{price} \\ \text{after-tax net income} \end{array} \quad = 8.75\%
$$

Our new after-tax cap rate is 8.75%.
Let's compare this with our old, before-tax cap rate:

$ 13,000	price	= 6.5%
$200,000	before-tax net income	

before-tax cap rate	6.5 %
after-tax cap rate	8.75%
increase in cap rate caused by tax benefits	2.25%

The building's cap rate jumped from 6.5 percent, without the tax savings, to 8.75 percent with the savings. This means that when the tax benefits available to John because of his bracket are added in, the building's available yield jumps by more than a third. Many readers may be puzzled at this point, however, because neither 6.5 percent nor 8.75 percent seem to be very good returns in today's market.

But remember that John is also concerned with debt return on mortgage and with appreciation, as well as with an annual return on his investment. John hopes the property will appreciate over the years, and that eventually his return and profit will come from selling for much more than he paid.

Nevertheless, we are not yet finished with after-tax yield. Let's now consider what the tax benefits do once we factor in mortgaging.

On the office building, the mortgage payments are $12,000 a year. It so happens that the owner is willing to carry back a mortgage for $150,000 at only 7.5 percent interest. (I've seen stranger things in today's market!) John must raise $50,000 cash as a down payment.

As we saw earlier, adding in the $12,000 mortgage payment brings the total expenses (before depreciation) up to $19,000. Since total revenue is $20,000, the building only produces $1,000 positive cash flow. John's cash flow on his $50,000 investment, therefore, is minimal. Adding the $4,500 from his tax savings, the true cash flow to John (given his tax bracket) is now 11 percent. That's the amount that he will earn on his money annually.

$$\frac{\$ 5,500}{\$50,000} = 11 \text{ percent}$$

USING THE AFTER-TAX CASH FLOW

Once John has found the after-tax cash flow, or true annual yield on his capital invested, there are two ways he can use it.

The first way is to compare this yield against a possible return from other investments. How does 11 percent cash flow stack up against what money-market funds, T-bills, leasing, research and development, cattle feeding and other tax-sheltered investments are paying? Does it make sense, from a return viewpoint, to buy the office building?

The second way is to compare this after-tax cash flow with the potential return from other office buildings. By this method, the building with the highest after-tax cash flow (assuming similar investment and risks) indicates the best investment. The building that John is considering will yield 11 percent. What about the building down the street? What about the one across town? We can re-apply the principles of the last chapter now using the after-tax cash flow.

Tax Risk

It should be noted that the after-tax cash flow is not a panacea. There are many other factors, such as tax risk, to consider. The after-tax cash flow we've projected for John presumes he'll remain in the 50 percent tax bracket, and that the building will remain occupied at its present level. Additional vacancies or John's dropping into a lower tax bracket would seriously affect the yield.

Therefore, to return to the point with which we began this chapter, an investment building must make good economic sense *before* the tax considerations. Does this one?

Income is $20,000 and expenses are $19,000, leaving a margin of only $1,000, or five percent. The dangers are vacancies or unexpected repairs. If either rises above $1,000 a year, the building cannot support itself. Of course, we're talking here about the down-side risk in hard times. Is five percent, or $1,000, enough to see the building through?

The answer can only be determined on a case-by-case basis. The investor has to consider the local and national economic climate, the location and physical condition of the building, the likelihood of continued or improved rental demand, and any other factor affecting the building's ability to produce income.

Yes, with a good building in a good area in good times, five percent is more than enough.

No, with a run-down building in a declining area facing a recession, five percent is not nearly enough.

What I'm getting at is a rule that must be understood when dealing with real estate: Expenses generally are either fixed or rising, but income is variable. What this means is that, to be economically sound, the property must have enough margin in *before-tax benefits* that it can handle income slippage against fixed expenses.

Taxes are not benefits, they are costs. Tax shelters don't mean you're making more money; they mean you're paying less taxes. In other words, you must have taxable income before you can benefit from a tax shelter. Without income, all the tax benefits in the world will do you no good. This, ultimately, is the reason that the property must make economic sense before the tax incentives are considered.

Chapter Five

RAISING CAPITAL FOR REAL ESTATE

People buy property with other people's money.

The principle of leveraging is well known to real estate investors. When you buy a home, you rarely put more than twenty percent down. When a person buys investment real estate, 60 to 80 percent of the purchase money is often borrowed.

There are several good reasons for this:

1. Often, the investor simply doesn't have the necessary capital to make the purchase—without financing, 95 percent of all real estate transactions probably could not be made.

2. Borrowing money reduces the amount at risk—the risk to the investor who puts up only twenty percent of the money is far less than if he or she were to put up 100 percent.

3. Finally, lenders are always very careful about where they put their money. Securing financing insures that another interested party has looked at the deal and found the risk warranted.

So much for theory. In actual practice, we have two situations that investors are screaming about today. The first is the increasing difficulty of borrowing money in today's tight economy. "Where do we get financing?" is a common cry. Secondly, investors who bought property a year or two back with terrible financing, hoping to refinance out in the future, are now wondering what they can do in a market as bleak or bleaker than when they bought. Many such investors are on the verge of losing their property to foreclosure. Again, the cry is, "Where do we get good financing?"

Where indeed? In this chapter, we'll look for some sources of financing real estate. We'll consider both borrowing money and "taking in partners." Let's begin with the so-called "institutional lenders."

INSTITUTIONAL LENDERS

The term "institution" simply refers to the fact that the lender is large and makes it a business to handle real estate mortgages. Institutional lenders include banks, savings and loan associations, insurance companies, pension funds, and real estate investment trusts (REITS). We'll get into the requirements of each in a moment, but first let's cover some ground rules about institutional lenders.

1) *First mortgages only.* This is not a hard and fast rule, but is generally true. Most institutional lenders will only make loans if they can secure a first mortgage or trust deed. (As investors know, being "first" means that, in the event the borrower defaults, the lender is first to receive money in a foreclosure sale.)

There are exceptions. Savings and loan associations and banks will make "second" mortgages. Typically, however, banks and S&Ls set an upper limit on the amount they will lend—often 60 to 80 percent of value on investment property on a first.

Sometimes, however, when an existing first mortgage on the property has a lower interest rate than the current rate, it can be advantageous for the borrower to keep the existing mortgage and get a new second. But regardless of whether the lender is making a first mortgage or a second, the *total* amount of money borrowed normally cannot exceed 60 to 80 percent of value. Savings and loan associations are a good source of funds for second mortgages. Some S&Ls actually *prefer* second mortgages, because they generally carry higher interest rates than firsts and last for shorter periods of time, often three to five years, which allows the S&L a good yield with a quick recovery.

2) *The property must qualify.* With homes, the typical means of qualifying for a mortgage is to show that *you* can make the payments. (Often, this means proving that, after other long-term debts, you earn three to four times the monthly payment—including principal, interest, taxes and insurance.) With investment property, the property must qualify. The rental income from the property must be sufficient to cover the principal and interest, plus all other operating expenses. This leads us to a third rule.

3) *Institutional lenders will not lend on negative cash flow.* As we'll see, much investment property today has negative cash flow (the expenses exceed the income), and institutional lenders will not lend on negative. They'll reduce the amount they will loan (and thereby the monthly payments) until the cash flow turns positive (they prefer a five percent margin); then they'll lend that amount.

If our property has an income of $25,000 a year and expenses of $10,000 before mortgage (such as taxes, insurance, maintenance and management), what is the maximum amount that a lender is likely to loan?

$25,000	income (after vacancy factor)
10,000	fixed expenses
$15,000	available cash for mortgage debt

Let's assume that the going interest rate is 14 percent. Our lender simply refers to a mortgage-table book to find that, at 14 percent, $15,000 a year ($1,250 a month) means a maximum mortgage of $106,000. That becomes the maximum loan.

But, let's say the selling price is $200,000. We want an 80 percent mortgage, or $160,000, so we ask the lender to increase the loan to 80 percent of sales price.

Our lender, however, will probably say, "At $160,000, the monthly mortgage payment for a thirty-year loan would be roughly $23,000. That's $8,000 more than your cash flow. You can't make the payments out of the building's income; so we won't make the mortgage. Our figures tell us that the maximum amount you can afford to pay is $15,000. At the current 14 percent rate, that means a maximum loan of $106,000, *regardless of what the sales price is*. On this property, we'll lend only 53 percent of value because of the cash-flow situation."

You can argue all you want, pointing out that your "after-tax" cash flow is positive, but it won't make any difference. The property has to carry its own weight.

There is another side to this coin, of course. If the asking price were only $100,000 and the cash flow remained the same, would the lender still loan $106,000—$6,000 more than a sales price? No. In that case, the maximum loan would probably be 75 to 80 percent. Under few circumstances will institutional lenders do better than that.

Given these rules, *where* do we go to find institutional mortgages?

As we'll see shortly, we can contact each lender, bank or S&L individually. But this is time consuming, difficult and in some cases impossible (since insurance companies, pension funds, REITS, some banks and savings and loans distant from our locale won't talk directly to individual borrowers). To get to the institutional lender we need an intermediary—a go-between who has all the contacts. This person is a *mortgage banker*.

"Mortgage banker" is sometimes confused with "mortgage broker," about whom we'll talk in a moment. Here's the difference. A mortgage banker advances money directly from his own funds, then sells the mortgage to an institutional lender. A mortgage broker acts as an agent for a lender. He doesn't advance money directly but charges a commission for putting lender and borrower together. These definitions are not as neat as they sound, however. Mortgage bankers sometimes act as agents, and mortgage brokers sometimes advance their own money.

Mortgage bankers often are listed in the yellow pages of your phone book (if not, check with local real estate brokers to find one). There are thousands of them across the country, and they are becoming the best source for financing in the United States today. Most handle residential property exclusively, but many also have an investment division.

A mortgage banker can help you borrow money by quickly telling you how big a loan you can get given your expense/income ratio; by quickly telling you who's lending now, at what interest rate, and up to what amounts; and by getting the money for you at no more points (a point is one percent of the loan amount) than if you went directly to the lender.

Mortgage bankers sometimes get a fee from the lender but mostly make their money by collecting the monthly payments—called "servicing the loan." The mortgage banker is your pipeline to institutional lenders offering money in your area.

Now that we know the general rules for institutional funds and a way of getting access to those funds, let's consider each lender individually:

Commercial and Mutual Savings Banks

These are a good source of investment financing. They will, however, loan only about 70–75 percent of their estimate of value, and they may insist on stiff interest rates. Going through a bank can be a trying experience, but in times of tight money, banks are among the few places with cash to loan.

Insurance Companies

Insurance companies always look for good investment property to lend money on. They do, however, have certain criteria which many investors do not like or want. Insurance companies usually look for the "long haul"—they want to see their money loaned out for decades. This makes sense, if we think about it. Insurance companies are committed to long-term insurance policies, and they want to match their investments to the term of their commitment.

This approach often results in something called a "locked-in mortgage," where the terms of the loan may *prevent* you from early payoff. You may be "locked in" to keeping that mortgage for 10, 15 or 20 years, which can be a decided disadvantage if you're trying to refinance to get cash out or to sell. At their option, insurance companies may not enforce the lock-in clause, but they usually do this only when they see a benefit to them. Such benefits include handling the refinancing themselves at a higher interest rate, or having the owner (or borrower) pay a stiff bonus for the privilege of paying off the mortgage early.

Because of frequent turnover, insurance companies seldom fool around with small pieces of property. They want properties that will bring in strong income for many years. Generally speaking, insurance companies stay away from non-residential property unless the mortgage amount is at least $500,000.

Pension Funds

There are thousands of pension funds across the country that are faced with a problem most of us wish we had—what to do with too much money. Each day, more money comes pouring into these funds from contributors.

The fund managers must invest that money prudently, so that it will grow and be available when the beneficiaries want to claim it. But what can these managers invest in? Stocks have been lackluster for years, and bonds have recently seen forty-year lows. T-bills and other short-term money certificates have been giving high returns, but they tend to fluctuate up and down. (They are a good place for holding money when rates are high, but for the long term, they are not that useful.) Where is the poor money manager going to place these funds? (Remember, by law, he or she has to invest it "prudently," which usually lets out large investments in rarities, bullion, and most other hard assets.)

The answer that many fund managers have found is real estate. Investment real estate has a long history of price appreciation, and is usually considered a prudent investment.

Pension-fund managers generally will lend on large pieces of real estate, in much the same way that insurance companies will. Pension-fund managers, however, sometimes want a piece of the action, and they may lend only if they can take an equity position as well. Nevertheless, they remain an important source of funds for investment property.

Real Estate Investment Trusts

Real Estate Investment Trusts (REITS) are another source of financing for investment real estate. These came into prominence during the early 1970s both as buyers and investors in real estate. They almost sank from sight during the recession of 1974–75 but have recently reemerged. Most of the REITS which have been successful have been equity REITS—they are like giant corporations which invest in property. But some mortgage REITS, which make money by lending, have begun to reappear.

Savings and Loan Associations

As of this writing, more than half the S&Ls in the country are hurting. They are paying out more money in withdrawals than they receive in deposits—a process called "disintermediation." This means they must sell their outstanding mortgages for cash to pay off depositors, and more importantly, it means they have little money to lend out. But times may get better for them. And although the overall picture is grim, individual savings and loans here and there—those with superior management—are thriving. It is still possible to get mortgage financing from these "islands in the storm."

NON-INSTITUTIONAL LENDERS

Mortgage Brokers

In many states, real estate brokers act as agents for lenders, in addition to acting as agents for buyers and sellers. These lenders, however, are not usually the institutional lenders we've just been speaking of. Typically, these lenders are individuals.

Individuals often have excess money they want to invest wisely—the amount could be a few thousand or a few hundred thousand, or even millions. These individuals may feel that real estate presents a good investment opportunity, from a mortgage viewpoint.

Foregoing the hassle and expense of advertising, dealing directly with borrowers, and so forth, these individual lenders deal with mortgage brokers. They tell the broker how much they have to lend at what rate and term, and on what kind of property they want to make the loan, and the mortgage broker finds a borrower to match the lender's needs. The lender makes the loan, and the mortgage broker charges a commission from either lender, borrower, or both.

In some states, mortgage brokerage is big business. In California, for example, when usury laws were lifted in the late 1970s, numerous mortgage-brokerage companies exploded into multi-hundred-million-dollar corporations. They made their money on commissions, on fees for collecting monthly payments, and on fees for late payments.

There was a big upset in the industry in the early 1980s, however, as many borrowers went into foreclosure due to loss of employment or other adverse economic conditions. Some mortgage brokers had "guaranteed" their lenders that they would make good on the payments, even if the borrowers couldn't. When many borrowers went into default, some mortgage brokers couldn't make good on their guarantees and went into bankruptcy. Nevertheless, mortgage brokers are still around. They tend to advertise heavily in papers and in the yellow pages, and they are not hard to locate.

Rules for Mortgage Brokers

First, seconds, or others. Mortgage brokers can often arrange financing on first, seconds, or even higher mortgages. It all depends on whether they can find a lender willing to go along with your project.

Maximum loan amount. Generally speaking, mortgage brokers won't arrange financing for more than 80 percent of *their* appraisal of property value. Sometimes, mortgage brokers are a bit more generous in appraising property than institutional lenders. After all, institutional lenders are loaning their own money and are naturally conservative. Mortgage bankers, on the other hand, are lending someone else's money, and they get a commission only if they make a loan.

Short-term, high interest rate. Individual lenders get into real estate because they want a higher yield on their money than they can get by investing in T-bills, money-market funds and the like. Short-term, high interest rates provide the necessary incentive for them to lend their money. For the borrower, that means the cost of money from a mortgage broker will be higher than from an institutional lender or mortgage banker. Additionally, there probably will be more points to pay. Still, they are a good source for funds, because they *will* often make second mortgages where institutional lenders won't.

No negative cash flow. Like their institutional counterparts, mortgage brokers rarely advise their lenders to make loans on property with negative cash flows. It simply wouldn't make sense. In the event of default and foreclosure, the lender who took the property back probably couldn't refinance to get the cash out in a negative situation.

Seller Financing

One of the most popular methods of securing financing in today's market is to have the seller of the property handle it. After all, who could be more motivated? In addition, there are tax incentives for the seller. Often when a seller disposes of a piece of investment property—an office building, industrial park or whatever—he or she will realize a hefty profit, and there may be large taxes, despite capital gains, to pay on the profit.

One way to defer paying that tax is to take back a mortgage, creating an installment sale. Under an installment sale (assuming the transaction otherwise qualifies), as long as the seller takes payment in at least two different years, he or she need only declare the taxable gain *as it is received.* This last is critical. If the seller doesn't receive the gain for ten years, the tax needn't be paid until then.

Look at it this way. The seller has an equity in an industrial park of $400,000. She accepts $100,000 cash down, and the buyer takes over the $300,000 balance on the existing mortgage.

$400,000	seller's equity
100,000	down payment
$300,000	balance due seller

If the seller takes this $300,000 in cash, he or she must pay tax on it that year. Assuming the top bracket and capital gains, the tax will be 20 percent, or $60,000. That's a lot to pay. But, if the seller takes the $300,000 in the form of a mortgage, then tax is only paid on the principal returned each year. As we've noted, in the early years, principal return is insignificant.

Some sellers willingly, even insistently, take on an interest-*only* mortgage, which is a way of deferring taxes far into the future. The advantage here is that *no* principal is paid back until the mortgage comes due, perhaps five or ten years down the road. With no principal coming due, *no taxes* are paid on the gain.

Sellers will consider carrying mortgages to get a sale and some tax advantages, but, there are some rules to seller financing (or lack of rules in this case).

No maximum amount. There is no maximum amount that a seller might carry back. A seller can carry any percentage of the financing.

No fees or points. Since the seller is advancing the money to purchase the property in the form of paper (a mortgage), there are normally no lender fees or points to pay. The cheapest mortgage in terms of up-front costs is the seller mortgage.

Low interest rate—long term. As an inducement to buy, many lenders will offer lower-than-market interest rates. Additionally, to get the monthly payment down, they may take a longer term (seldom more than thirty years on a first, but frequently five to ten years on a second).

Financing negative cash flow. Unlike other lenders, sellers are often willing to finance negative cash flows, *if their mortgage is what puts the property into the negative position.* Their reasoning is simple. If they have to take the property back because the borrower/buyer can't make the payments, they're in the same position they were before they sold. Given that viewpoint, many sellers may hope that the borrower will default. Sellers are perhaps the only source for financing negative cash flow other than taking in partners, as we'll see shortly.

Seller Financing Over Existing Mortgages

One problem with seller financing is that sellers rarely own the property free and clear. What's to be done about the existing mortgage? Here are a variety of answers.

Assumptions. The most common way of handling this is for the buyer to assume the liability of the existing first mortgage, and for the seller to give a second.

Subject to. In some cases, particularly in states where the "due on sale" clause in the mortgage is enforceable—meaning the lender can demand all the loan money at once if there's a sale—some buyers purchase "subject to," which means that the original seller retains liability under the mortgage. This may circumvent the "due on sale" clause. Check with your broker or attorney.

Wraparound. Finally, the seller can give the buyer/borrower a "wrap," which usually yields a higher return for the seller. Here the *seller* retains liability for the first, and the borrower makes just one payment—larger than the sale price. The seller then takes out sufficient money from the payment to pay the monthly on the first and keeps the balance as his return on the money loaned.

Typical wrap		
$200,000	existing first	12 percent interest
+100,000	equity to be given to buyer as mortgage	14 percent interest
$300,000	total wrap yield to seller	14 percent interest

In the above wrap, the seller receives 14 percent interest on $300,000. However, the seller is only advancing $100,000. After the seller pays the 12 percent interest on the existing $200,000 mortgage, there is still 2 percent interest left on that money. That goes into the seller's pocket, giving him or her a higher yield on the $100,000 actually loaned.

Existing Lender Financing

An excellent but often overlooked method of financing is to have the existing lenders advance additional monies. This can be considered from two viewpoints:

When purchasing the property: This is the simplest application. The buyer (perhaps in conjunction with the seller) calls the lender of existing financing on the property directly. The buyer proposes that the lender increase the amount loaned on the property.

The lender might agree to such a proposal if there were an incentive. There are three possible incentives that a new buyer/ borrower can offer:

1. "If you will increase the loan amount (advance new monies to help me buy), I will increase the interest rate on the existing mortgage." (The alternative is to have the buyer take over the existing mortgage, with the seller continuing to get the old, presumably lower, rate.) This is a big incentive.

2. "If you will increase the loan amount, I will pay you a one-time fee." This has the effect, again, of increasing the yield to the lender.

3. "If you don't agree to advance more money, the seller will default and lose the property. You'll have to take over the property to protect your position." This can be an excellent motivation if the seller is indeed going to lose the property. *In weak markets, lenders do not want to take back property.*

When already owning the property: The second application occurs when we've bought the property, and we want to refinance to get more money out, or we are in trouble and need to renegotiate the financing. This often occurs today when buyers take over existing financing which has balloon payments coming due. Often, second or third mortgages are paid interest only, which means that the monthly payment just goes to service the interest. The principal all comes due at a fixed date—usually three to five years after the mortgage is made.

Sometimes we own property and these due dates are upon us. We can't get institutional financing to get out, and other sources may be equally closed to us. Another alternative is to approach the lender. We can use some similar rules:

1. "If you will extend the loan term, I will pay you a higher interest rate."

2. "If you will extend the loan term, I will pay you a one-time fee."

3. "If you don't extend the loan term, I'll lose the property and you'll be stuck with it." This has an additional motivational force in that, if we go into bankruptcy (depending on the type of bankruptcy we file) at the same time we go into mortgage default, the property could be tied up for two years or more. During that time, the lender may not be able to sell or even rent the property. This is an extraordinary, but highly effective, motivation. See your attorney.

4. In addition, there are other techniques which can be used in a situation where we, as owners, are faced with losing the property through foreclosure. We can ask the lender for example, if he or she would take part ownership in the property for extending the term. "If you will extend the term, I will give you half the equity in the property." The incentive in this offer is that the lender will continue to have the mortgage as well as part ownership of the equity, but we will continue to carry *the management headache*.

This works best when the property is not currently in default, and the mortgage still has a few months to run. If we're already in default, it doesn't amount to much of an offer since the lender's going to be the full owner in a short time anyhow.

5. We can ask the lender, "What are you going to do with the money when I pay off the mortgage I owe you?" (This works, really, only with non-institutional lenders.) Depending on what the lender plans to do with the money, we might strike a bargain. If the lender is planning to reloan it, why not relend it to us on this property?

If the lender intends to buy another property, we might trade out of our present property into partnership with the lender in a mutually owned property (we put up our equity; the lender puts up the mortgage amount). There are tax advantages for both of us here, and together we may be able to purchase a bigger piece of property than either of us could purchase separately.

If the lender plans to buy a car or other personal property, perhaps we can buy the car ourselves, using our property as collateral, and give the car to the lender for releasing the mortgage. And so on. The key here is to tie our property to whatever the lender wants from the money, and the only limitation is our own creativity.

Partner Financing

This works whether we're in a situation of buying or one of refinancing, and involves splitting up the equity in the property among several partners. The most common form of partner financing is the limited partnership.

Limited Partnerships. As investors in real estate know, a limited partnership is a legal association in which partners contribute money to buy a piece of property. All of the partners participate in the profits and tax benefits.

They don't, however, all share in the liability. In a limited partnership, there are two classes of partner. The *general partner* is fully obligated and responsible in the same way that an individual property owner is. The *limited partner* is obligated only in terms of the money he or she puts up and so can lose only the money he or she invests (or may be committed to).

This has important ramifications. If the property goes into foreclosure, the lender may be able to sue the partnership, and sometimes the general partner, for any deficiency on the foreclosure sale. But the lender can't get money out of the limited partners unless they personally signed the mortgage. The limited partners have such limited liability in the partnership that they can rarely be successfully sued for a personal injury on the property. In order to protect their limited liability, however, limited partners generally must not become involved in the direct management of the property. The general partner does that.

The limited partnership is a device that can be used to raise money by almost anyone who can satisfy the legal requirements. We become a general partner, for example—after having an attorney set up the partnership and explain the legal and tax ramifications—and take in limited partners who put up money. We may or may not put up money, but we find, buy, manage, and eventually sell the property.

If we need $100,000 in cash as a down payment—or to meet a balloon payment, or to refinance our equity—we might take in five partners. Each of them would put up $20,000 and become limited partners. For their equity, they would get a share of ownership, which could be any amount agreed upon. They could split the full ownership, for example, each getting twenty percent. Or they could split half the ownership, each getting 10 percent.

By using the limited partnership, we can raise money and yet retain control. We can raise enough money, in effect, to finance 100 percent of the purchase price. The drawback to limited partnerships, however, is that we must give up equity, and we must split the profits when the property is sold.

Small limited partnerships—originated by individual investors who want a property too big for them to buy alone—are put together every day. Each state has specific laws allowing this. These laws, however, usually limit the size of such partnerships. In California, for example, such a "friendly" limited partnership generally cannot have more than ten partners, and the general partner may not contact more than 25 people in soliciting partners (called the 10/25 rule). Other states are different. If creating a general partnership appeals to you, you should check with an accountant or attorney in your area. My recent book, *Riches in Real Estate* (McGraw-Hill, 1981), is about how individuals can form such limited partnerships to raise capital.

Why would a person want to be a limited partner and give up control? A few of the many good reasons are: no management headaches, limited liability, small investment, and a chance for good profit.

If, however, you're considering investing in real estate as a limited partner because these benefits appeal to you, you should heed a few words of caution. Not all limited-partnership ventures are successful—unscrupulous general partners can bilk limited partners; the property can be economically unsound; the IRS can deny write-offs; and a lot more unexpected or unwanted things can happen. Before you get involved in a limited partnership, have your personal financial advisor check it out.

Venture Capital

"Venture capital" is the last method of raising equity capital we'll consider. The reason we're considering it last is because it's tricky and expensive.

There are groups of investors across the country who have formed venture-capital organizations. They seek out good properties and individuals who want to buy them but don't have the cash. Then they put up a part of the money in exchange for an equity position. Venture capital shouldn't be confused with financing. In financing, the lender gains a mortgage; in venture capital, you gain both a mortgage and a partner.

Typically, venture-capital organizations want a portion of the equity plus a mortgage on the amount loaned. For example, let's say we're buying a shopping center, and we need to come up with a million dollars in cash for the down payment. We have $500,000 and need a half-million more. The venture capitalists might offer us the other $500,000 in a mortgage but insist on *three-quarters ownership*.

Outrageous? Maybe. But if it's a good enough deal, we might jump at it. Let's say that the shopping center was grossly underpriced, and we raised rents the minute we bought it. Right away its value jumped a million dollars. Of that new million, three-fourths would go to the venture people, but one-fourth, or $250,000 would go to us. That's an overnight, fifty percent profit on our own $500,000, which we might not otherwise make. You bet we'd go for it.

Finding venture capital, quite frankly, is very hard. But there are ways. Investment-finance divisions of large real estate companies often know where to find it. Sellers sometimes know. But, if you haven't any leads, the "commercial finance" department of a large bank is a good place to start.

Banks lend money to businesses in their commercial finance departments. These are collateralized loans covering inventory—they don't involve real property. But, very often, the people in commercial finance deal directly with people in venture capital; so an officer in a bank's commercial finance department may be able to lead you to people who have venture capital to lend.

These, then, are some of the ways to raise capital. In the remaining chapters of this book, we'll see how these are applied, and we'll come across several others. I think the final point here should be that the only measure of how much you can raise is your own creativity and daring. If you can find the right people to ask and are willing to take sensible, calculated risks, you probably can raise the money you need to buy any property.

Chapter Six

CONDOMINIUM CONVERSION FOR BIG BUCKS

There really are only three ways to invest in a condominium (or co-op—much of this chapter about condos also applies to co-operatives). The simplest way is to buy a condominium unit, rent it out for a period of time, and then sell it for a profit. The other ways are to build a condominium project and then sell for profit, or to buy an apartment building, *convert* to condominiums, and then sell for profit. What we'll concern ourselves with is finding an existing apartment building and then converting it to a condominium project. A condominium project need not be large—a four-unit building will do. Of course, with larger units there is more opportunity for profit, as well as a greater need for investment capital. In any case, there's a lot of money to be made in condo conversion.

CONDO CONVERSION MAY BE
THE HOTTEST DEAL IN TOWN

Jerry, a beginning investor who'd had some success with land, was ready to try bigger and better things. He noticed that a great many apartment buildings were being converted to condominiums in his area of the city. He had heard that condo conversion offered big opportunities, and he wondered how the profit was being made.

Jerry went to visit a recent conversion—the Day-More Terrace—and found that former two-bedroom apartment units of modest size were being offered for sale at about $100,000 apiece. He was shocked. Jerry's aunt had lived in the same building not more than a year ago, and she had paid only $350 a month in rent for the same unit. Was a $350-a-month apartment worth $100,000? When Jerry asked the salesperson, he was told that apparently it was. The project had 20 units, of which 14 already had sold in a period of two months.

Jerry was intrigued by the fast-paced sales. At $100,000 a crack, the 20 units would bring in $2,000,000. That was a lot of money for an apartment building that could rent its units for only $350 each. If he could just figure out how it was done, Jerry felt he could take advantage of such an opportunity on a similar building. The real estate salesperson was unable to answer his more detailed questions regarding the building and the conversion. She referred him to the property owners, the Getmore Construction Company.

Getmore, Jerry quickly discovered, was owned by Sally and Beatrice, two sisters who had been in the real estate business for some time. He called and made an appointment to talk with them at a convenient time. When he arrived, Jerry explained that he wanted to invest in a conversion but didn't know the "ins" and "outs" of the business. He hoped they could help. Sally seemed quite busy, but Beatrice said she'd be happy to help. Beatrice said that she and Sally had bought the Day-More Terrace Apartments for one million dollars, and she showed Jerry how the price had been calculated.

DAY-MORE CONVERSION APARTMENT
BUILDING EVALUATION

unit rent	$	350
total units	×	20
total monthly income		7,000
	×	12
annual gross income		84,000
multiplier	×	12
price		$1,008,000

"We had to come up with 25 percent in cash, or $250,000," Beatrice began. "We obtained a loan for the balance of $750,000. We bought the place and then went through the process of applying for the right to convert. There were maps to file with the city and state, subdivision laws to comply with, and an environmental impact report to file. We also had to help relocate tenants who chose to move instead of buying their units.

"The paperwork alone cost us $30,000 and two years in time. Then and only then could we begin the conversion. The city required one and a half off-street parking spaces for each condo unit, but the building had been zoned for apartment usage with only one car per unit. So we had to come up with ten more parking spaces. If we hadn't been able to convert the big vacant area at the back of the lot to parking, we'd have been forced to reduce the number of condo units we could sell.

"We repainted the building inside and out, then put all new stoves, ovens, dishwashers, and garbage disposals in each unit. We installed a new central-water-heating, air-conditioning and space-heating system. We refurbished the pool heater and filter and overhauled the elevator machinery. We even put on a new roof. And I'm sure we did a lot more that I can't remember right now. The refurbishing cost us $200,000. Here's a sheet of our estimated expenses."

CONVERSION EXPENSES

paperwork	$ 30,000
relocation costs	25,000

refurbishing	200,000
sales commission to sell	
20 units, including closing costs	30,000
lost rent while apartments were	
being converted	42,000
other costs	25,000
	$352,000

"Do you mean you had to raise an additional $352,000 in cash just to complete this project?" Jerry asked incredulously.

"No," Beatrice continued, "we arranged an interim loan for $400,000. It was a kind of intermediate financing that covered the cost of the conversion, as well as the cost of the original loan, until the units could be sold and everyone paid back. There was an additional $200,000 in interest on that loan."

Jerry whistled. "That didn't leave you much, did it?"

Beatrice looked curiously at Jerry and said, "It all depends on how you look at it."

After Jerry thanked Beatrice and left her office, he took out a piece of paper and calculated Beatrice and Sally's profit on the apartment building.

PROFIT ON DAY-MORE

amount realized from sale of 20 units			$2,000,000
less costs	purchase price	$1,000,000	
	conversion expense	352,000	
	additional interest	200,000	
		$1,552,000	1,552,000
profit			$ 448,000

Jerry whistled again when he saw the last figure. They had made nearly half a million dollars in profit on their initial investment of $250,000. Not bad for about two years' work.

Why the Profit Potential

Jerry realized, of course, that not all conversions would do as well, but he wondered why any did well at all. Why was it that an apartment, which in this case rented for only $350 a month, could sell for as much as $100,000? He contacted Leonard, an old friend who had been a real estate broker for many years.

Leonard listened patiently as Jerry explained the entire financial history of the Day-More apartments. Then Leonard said, "It's a matter of switching markets. That's how the profit is made." Leonard smiled when Jerry indicated that he didn't understand.

Leonard showed Jerry how single-family housing was evaluated, pointing out the comparison of recent sales to determine price. Then he said, "In the area of Day-More, I would assume that single-family homes are selling for $150,000 or more, and I know that new condominiums in the area are bringing in about $110,000. It's a highly desirable section of the city. Other homes and condos are the comparables for the Day-More. Given the values I've just mentioned, it's easy to see why the Day-More is selling so quickly for $100,000 a unit.

"On the other hand," Leonard continued, "the rental market in this area is far different. Most renters around here are young couples or retired folks who can't pay much more than $350 a month. Plus, there's a strict rent-control law in the city that prevents dramatic rent increases; so $350 is probably all the former owner of the Day-More could get."

Leonard then reminded Jerry that income is the basis for evaluating investment property. With the relatively low income of Day-More, even with a multiplier of 12, a price of $1,000,000 was not unreasonable.

"You see," Leonard concluded, "as an apartment building, the place really isn't worth more than one million dollars. But, as a condominium building, it's worth twice that price. The difference comes from its *use*. The profit that Sally and Beatrice made came from changing the use of the land. They changed it from a low-yielding use to a high one. It's as simple as that."

Jerry understood—it was indeed obvious. Even the term "conversion" indicated a change in usage. "Find a new use and make a profit," Leonard added. "That's an old slogan in real estate and one well worth remembering. It's made a lot of people lots of money."

Jerry had seen where the profit was made and why, and a few months later, he found a suitable apartment building, bought it, and started conversion. Two years later, when his last unit was sold, his profit exceeded that of Beatrice and Sally at Getmore!

HOW TO DO IT

Of course, it's not all that simple. Here's a list of things that every converter must be aware of and deal with:

1. Find an appropriate property.
2. Convince lenders to go along.
3. Convince government agencies to permit the conversion (including adapting the plan to meet any changes they demand).
4. Handle the needs of tenants who are forced to move by the project.
5. Determine what type of physical changes to the property are necessary.
6. Sell the finished units in a market two to three years in the future, when demand, interest rates and competition are unknown.

Finding an Appropriate Property

Finding a suitable apartment building to convert to condominiums is often much harder than it sounds. Most investors ask, "Should I look for the building first and then see if the neighborhood is appropriate? Or should I find a good neighborhood and then try to get the right building?" The answer is that both courses must be followed simultaneously.

Ideally, the investor will find a highly desirable residential section of a city, where there is a shortage of available, single-family homes. In such areas, older apartment buildings become prime targets as investment opportunities. Once an apartment building has been found, whatever its size, the investors must determine the feasibility of converting. The question becomes, "If I convert, can I sell and make a profit?" Surprisingly, we can get a good idea of the answer through a market analysis.

A *market* analysis is a close look at the real estate market in which the proposed condominium conversion would compete. It typically covers at least three areas: demand, competition, and examination of costs versus revenue to determine profit.

A *demand* analysis can be worked up by any local real estate consulting firm, or it can be handled directly by the investor. It involves seeking out existing condominium developments (as well as single-family home sales) and comparing the supply to the volume of sales. A demand-analysis sheet might look like this.

Building Location	Number of Units	Number Unsold	Average time from offering to sale
New Condominiums			
Magellan Apartments	20	15	2 months
Hirschorn Condos	80	10	6 months
Bel-Air Condos	73	3	5 months
Condo Conversions			
Snider Apartments	14	1	2 months
Leisure Time Condos	96	6	7 months
Borealis Condos	50	15	3 months
Home Resales	Volume Last Month	Volume Year Ago	
	157	133	

Although an actual demand-analysis sheet would include many more items, such as the features offered by each project—size, price, and so forth—we can at least see the method employed. We want to know what else is available in the area and how it's doing. The analysis above reports a fair number of both new and converted condo units in the area, which are selling in seven months or less. So we should expect to sell out any condos we are contemplating, all other factors being equal, within six months after completion.

The number of home sales is another indicator of strong demand in the area. Here, the volume of sales for the last month is running far ahead of the volume for the previous year, which indicates strong homeowner demand. (The volume of resales can usually be found by contacting the local real estate board.)

Once we know the demand is there, we must determine what the competition is like. We have some idea, of course, from our demand sheet. But we need a much more thorough analysis, particularly with regard to location and price. A competition-analysis sheet might look like this:

COMPETITON-ANALYSIS SHEET

Building	No. of Units	Layout of Units Bedrooms/Bath		Prices	Median Price	Sq. Ft. Price	Fees/ Month
Magellan	20	1–2	1	$ 70–80,000	$ 75,000	$ 75	$ 27
Hirschorn	80	2	2	120–140,000	132,000	110	127
Bel-Air	73	1–3	2	130–155,000	135,000	122	50
Snider	14	2	1	80–90,000	95,000	119	63
Leisure Time	96	2	2	76–95,000	85,000	77	90
Borealis	50	2	1	65–85,000	75,000	75	30

In this chart, the median price is a figure above and below which half the units are priced. The square-foot price is arrived at by dividing the median price by the total number of square feet. The fees are typical monthly homeowner-association dues.

The competition-analysis sheet shows what nearby condominium projects are doing. It is broken down into those projects which are new and those which are conversions. We can expect new projects to sell for more than a conversion, since a conversion, after all, remains an old building, and this is borne out by the sheet. Looking at the square-foot cost, we quickly see that the majority of the conversions are priced lower than most of the new condos. The single exception is the Snider, which has a $119-square-foot price tag, among the highest. To be competitive, we must offer two-bedroom units with one or two baths at something between $75 and $119 per square foot. Now we need a more detailed comparison to cut down the leeway.

COMPARATIVE ANALYSIS SHEET

Features	Magellan	Hirschorn	Bel-Air	Snider	Leisure Time	Borealis	Our Building
swimming pool	no	yes	yes	yes	no	no	yes
view from each unit	no	no	yes	yes	no	no	yes
covered parking	no	yes	yes	yes	no	no	yes
elevator	no	no	yes	yes	yes	no	no
air cond.	yes	yes	yes	yes	yes	yes	no
central laundry	yes	yes	yes	yes	yes	yes	yes
patios	no	yes	yes	yes	no	no	yes
rec. room	no	yes	yes	yes	no	no	no
spa	no	yes	yes	yes	no	no	no
common lawn area	yes	yes	yes	yes	yes	yes	yes
security guard	no	yes	yes	yes	no	no	yes
condition	new	new	new	excellent	good	good	good
size of median unit (sq. ft.)	1,000	1,200	1,100	800	1,100	1,000	1,100

In the comparative analysis sheet we see how our building
stacks up against the others, feature by feature. Several things
are immediately obvious. The Snider building, for example,
charges so much because it offers every feature and is in excellent condition. This is offset, however, by the relatively small
size of its units.

Our building lacks an elevator, air conditioning (which all
the others have), a recreation room, and a spa. It does, however, have patios and a security guard, which our two closest
competitors—Leisure Time and Borealis—do not. From this
analysis, if we build air conditioning into our project, we can
probably justify charging close to $100 per square foot. That
would make us fairly competitive with other condos in the
area. Since our units have a median size of 1,100 square feet,
that means our median price could be $110,000.

If our analyses are correct—and considering the locations,
which we've assumed here to be equally desirable—we can
now determine whether or not there's any money to be made
in this project. We need to compare the amount of money we'll
receive from our condo project with the price.

PROFIT DETERMINATION ON THE BUILDING
WE ANTICIPATE CONVERTING

Income (30 units at $110,000) =	$3,300,000	
Income from rent until conversion is completed	200,000	
	$3,500,000	$3,500,000
Expenses		
Purchase price	$2,000,000	$2,940,000
Conversion costs	500,000	
Loan costs	300,000	
Closing costs	140,000	
	$2,940,000	$2,940,000
Profit		$ 560,000
Total cash investment to get into the project		$ 500,000

Return on investment—better than 100% over the estimated, two-and-a-half-year period to complete the project.

If our market analyses and estimates of conversion costs are correct, it appears, at this stage, that we can make considerable money by going ahead with this project. There are, however, many more hurdles to overcome.

Convincing Lenders to Go Along

In order to make this conversion worcn we will need to borrow a great deal of money. Though we have about half a million in cash, we need two million to buy the apartment building and almost another million for additional costs. That means we must finance roughly 2.4 million dollars, or 80 percent of the final price.

This isn't really as impossible as it may sound at first. Our initial loan is on the apartment building we buy. First, we put $500,000 down and assume an existing $1.5 million loan on the building we are buying. So, in reality, we are only getting 75 percent financing. Then we need to arrange for an additional $900,000 (plus another $100,000 we'll put up) to cover conversion and other costs. This money comes from something called "interim financing."

Interim financing is simply a loan that covers the extra money needed for the conversion. In a good money market (no shortage of funds for lending), 80% of the ultimate sales price is readily available in interim financing. During a "money crunch," or a tight money period, the available amount drops below 75%. One risk with condo conversion is that the market may have soured by the time we're ready to arrange for interim financing. (Getting a standby commitment from a lender helps here.)

The way interim financing works is quite simple. In our case, we need to borrow $2.4 million. Our interim financing could consist of a completely new loan for that amount, with the money issued as we incur expenses. Or, we may get the money in the form of an All Inclusive Trust Deed (AITD), in which case we would retain the existing loan on the building ($1.5 million), and the interim lender will come up with an additional $900,000. We'll make a single payment directly to the lender for the $2.4 million loan. The interim lender then pays off the first loan and keeps the balance for himself.

With a conversion, there are actually three types of loans:

- Apartment-building purchase—assume existing loan
- Conversion—arrange interim financing
- Sale—individual buyers arrange their own loans

As investors, we are responsible for arranging all the financing. Let's take it step by step.

There is some sort of financing on almost every building, and if it's assumable, we should check it out in detail. We want to know, for example, if there is a "pre-payment penalty"—a specific amount we must raise if we wish to pay off the loan before it's due.

Some loans, particularly those issued by insurance companies on large buildings, are "locked in," which means that no pre-payment is allowed. Sometimes the lender will unlock if we offer a cash bonus. But if the lender is unwilling to unlock, we'll probably have to abandon this particular project.

Interim financing is the most difficult to arrange, because the lender is taking a substantial risk. If we succeed, the lender's money is returned with high interest in a few years. But if we fail—if we can't sell the condo units—the lender will have to foreclose, taking back an apartment building that probably can't be rented for the payments. The investor/borrower has to do the most convincing with the interim lender. (Of course, if we have sufficient capital to carry us through the conversion, we can forget this step entirely.)

The interim lender is going to ask himself three questions about the investor and the project: (1) Does the investor have the expertise to complete a successful project? (2) Does the investor have the net worth to weather unforeseen difficulties that may arise? (3) Is the project itself likely to succeed? To help the interim lender (bank, S&L, insurance company, etc.) answer these questions, the investor presents a comprehensive loan package, usually with the aid of a mortgage banker.

Finally, there are permanent loans to the condo buyers, for which the investor makes the initial arrangements. The new buyer, who actually signs the papers and borrows the money, normally must commit to a permanent loan for at least 80% of the sales price. In the absence of such a commitment, the interim lender may not be willing to act. Also, the lender probably will hold back some money from the interim loan until a certain portion of the units are sold. The interim lender doesn't want the investor to reap any profit until the project appears certain to succeed.

Financing is perhaps the most complicated area of condominium conversion, and we've only brushed the surface here. But we've looked at some of the problems a potential conversion will face, and suggested some solutions. Any good mortgage banker can help you prepare a suitable package for the specific lender you're approaching.

Government Permission

In the good old days, converting an apartment building to a condominium only required an appearance before a planning commission board and the preparation of the proper documents. But things have changed considerably.

In most communities today, there are a great many regulations which must be met. A subdivision report, for example, generally must be filed. Why? A condominium is like a subdivision in miniature—a group of individual units to be separately owned—with all the units contained in one building. Permission to subdivide a building, in many states, must come from a state or county commission, and the process can take from six months to three years.

In some areas, an environmental impact report also must be filed. If there are to be any physical changes to the building, or if tenants are to be moved out and owners moved in (always the case in a conversion), then the report must explain how this will be handled.

In addition, many local governments have taken exception to condominium conversion. The plight of elderly tenants forced out of their apartments, whether by conversion or high rents, has resulted in a whole series of restrictive conversion laws across the country. Some cities have banned condominium conversion entirely, while others have imposed onerous conditions.

For example, one method of effectively reducing the number of conversions is to increase the off-street parking requirement. If the property has no excess land, and above-ground or subterranean parking is impossible, the investor's only alternative is to reduce the number of units. If an apartment building has 20 units and 20 parking places, but two parking places are required for each converted condo, then 20 units must be converted into 10. This means knocking out walls, enlarging rooms, putting in new doors, and so forth, not to mention lost profit. While this may be practical with a few buildings, on most it is not. Simply increasing the parking requirement can eliminate more than half of the proposed conversions within an area.

Handling the Needs of Dislocated Tenants

Although profit is the investor's ultimate goal in a conversion, the investor also has a moral responsibility to the former tenants in the building. After all, converting actually means uprooting those tenants who are unable or unwilling to buy the units they are in.

In the past, too many investors overlooked their responsibilities in this area. They simply bought an apartment building and gave the tenants 30-day notices to leave. These investors showed no regard for the inability of elderly, infirm, or ill tenants to move, or for the difficulty of finding other affordable rental space in the area.

As more conversions occurred, however, many investors recognized the problem and came up with programs to relocate former tenants in new apartments. They often allowed former tenants to remain where they were until new rental units could be found for them.

Nevertheless, the cries that conversions were forcing people into the streets became a political issue, and many local governments stepped in to write new relocation laws. Here is what a typical relocation law might require (compiled from the codes of several southwestern cities):

1. Tenants must be notified a minimum of *one year* in advance of conversion and must be given the right to purchase the unit they are in at no more than the advertised sales price.

2. Tenants shall be assisted in relocating to comparable housing according to the following factors: size, price, location, proximity to medical and recreation facilities (parks, community centers, shops, transportation, schools, churches and synagogues).

3. Until the tenant is relocated, he or she shall be allowed to remain in the old unit with no rental increases.

4. If no similar unit (as defined above) can be found and a more expensive unit must be rented, the *developer will pay* the cost of the difference between the new and the old rents for one year.

5. The developer will pay *all* the moving costs of the tenant, except that the developer may designate the moving company used. The move will be total and not require any assistance from the tenant (insurance, packing, boxing, transportation, etc., to be provided by the mover).

6. The developer will offer to pay a cash relocation fee to each tenant of $_____ (the amount is usually between $100 and $500).

While these new regulations provide a much needed burst of concern for the tenant, they can be exceedingly expensive to the investor. They can also be time-consuming, and time, when converting, can be very costly.

Anticipating the needs of tenants to be relocated and complying with governmental dictums on such relocation is an important consideration in the decision of whether or not to convert.

Determining Physical Changes to Property

Basically, there are two roads to travel in the physical conversion of an apartment building. The high road involves correcting all deficiencies in the building—including bad wiring, plumbing, air conditioning, elevator motors, pool pumps, bad roofs, and so forth. Unfortunately, much of the correction just noted is extremely expensive and doesn't show. Prospective condo purchasers won't know how much, if any, of this work was done, unless they request specific inspection reports (which few condo buyers do).

This has led many converters to seek the low road of cosmetic change—refacing the front of the building, painting it inside and out, replacing ovens and ranges, and any other changes that will be visibly noted by a prospective buyer. The idea is not to correct deficiencies, but simply to cover up everything with a flashy "new coat of paint." This kind of renovation is not so costly, and more important, all of it shows.

Which is the right path? Investors with a conscience will do both. They'll do the major work that should be done, and they'll also beautify the project. If the deal is put together properly, the initial purchase price will reflect any poor state of maintenance or repair. For example, if a building in good shape is worth $500,000, in poor shape it might sell for only $450,000. Instead of pocketing the $50,000 difference, the investor should use it for major repair work.

Before any purchase is made, it is vitally important that the investor have an excellent idea of the costs of any necessary renovation, along with estimates for increases due to inflation. The aid of good architects and building renovators is critical here—if the cost estimates of physical conversion are too low, the investor will have subsequent financial problems; if they are too high, a potentially successful project may get passed by.

Selling in an Unknown Future

The payoff for a condo conversion usually comes several years after the initial investment. This, essentially, is where the risk is greatest. If we can't sell our condo units two or three years down the road, regardless of how good our marketing survey once looked, we lose—badly. An awful lot of condominium investors have taken the gamble and had it pay off big. But there are a few who lost.

The rapid changes in today's market make predicting the future very difficult. Interest rates, credit, competition, and even the availability of buyers who can afford to purchase are almost totally unpredictable from one month to the next, let alone years into the future. Will we be able to sell our units years from now? We can't be certain, but if we have the daring to take a big plunge, a condo conversion could be the best and biggest bet in town.

Chapter Seven

THE CHALLENGE OF AN APARTMENT BUILDING

What's wrong with buying an apartment building as an investment today? Nothing, if you buy with the intention of converting to condominiums, or if you buy a high-rent, luxury apartment. But in today's market, in most areas, you could be in for trouble if you buy a middle-of-the-road, typical apartment building. The dream of owning an apartment building—and retiring on the income it provides—has faded.

WHAT HAPPENED TO THE MARKET?

In order to understand today's apartment-building dilemma, it's important to appreciate how we got here.

In the late 1950s and early 1960s, I was actively involved in selling smaller apartment buildings in California, and I recall the great difficulty we had in moving the investments. There were duplexes, four-plexes, six-plexes, 10- and 20-unit buildings, on up to hundred-unit projects in every urban and suburban area. The apartment-building market was clearly overbuilt—there simply weren't enough tenants to fill all the units.

In those days, the typical rent for an apartment was between $75 and $150 a month, which was considered a lot of money. In order to fill their units many owners offered tenants a month or more rent-free. This led to a situation where certain unscrupulous tenants would hop from one building to the next to get as much free rent as they could. Builders who put up the structures on speculation—hoping to sell them to investors—were desperate. They simply could not fill the buildings, and without income from tenants the buildings couldn't attract investors.

Eventually, rents went down. In a typical, fully rented, 11-unit building, the total monthly income was about $1100, and the expenses—a mortgage at six percent interest, taxes, and insurance—were about $900. That left only a $200 monthly profit before vacancies and maintenance were considered. Given the lack of tenants and their high mobility, vacancy and maintenance costs were often high enough to lead to a negative cash flow for the building's owner. Prospective investors weren't much interested.

I vividly recall long blocks of unsalable apartment buildings which desperate builders were offering for *free*! This meant, of course, that the buyer would simply have to assume the current financing. The banks and S&Ls, which had put up the money for the construction, were willing to convert construction loans to long-term financing for anyone who would assume ownership. An investor only had to sign on the dotted line that he or she would be responsible for making the loan payments. Yet, few investors took the bait.

It really didn't make sense to buy in those days—you had to make mortgage payments that were relatively high, fight to keep tenants, work hard to maintain the building, and, in the end, come up with money out of your own pocket just to make ends meet. Who'd want an investment like that, particularly when the situation didn't seem likely to improve?

How did this oversupply come about? Why did builders construct all those buildings if they knew they wouldn't sell? They didn't know, of course. But, more important, it made sense to build apartments. In the 1960s, in many parts of the country, good, close-in land was readily available at relatively inexpensive prices; building materials were plentiful and cheap; and the cost of labor was not prohibitive. And many builders discovered an interesting fact—they could get a construction loan (a short-term mortgage issued for the exclusive purpose of paying for building construction) that would help produce 110% financing! It actually was possible to make a profit simply by building and then letting the mortgage company take the property back in foreclosure. (This, of course, was a one-time affair. Once you went down as a builder, no one would lend you money.)

Jake was a builder in those days who knew an opportunity when he saw one. He found a suitable piece of land on which to construct an eight-unit building and offered $10,000 for the property—$2,000 in cash and a subordinated second mortgage for the remaining $8,000. (A "subordinated second" was a device whereby the landowner agreed that his $8,000 mortgage would be second in line to a construction loan on the property. This was necessary, since the builder could only get a construction loan if the lender were assured of being first in line on the property.)

Once he secured control of the land, Jake put together a package for the lender specifying construction costs. Jake "padded" his estimate by including extra costs that wouldn't really materialize. "If the lender doesn't care," Jake argued, "why should I?"

The loan was made and the building constructed, and Jake discovered that his padding amounted to $9,000. This was cash left over after the project was completed, offsetting his outlay for the land by $7,000. If he could just sell the building, or even give it away, Jake thought, he could keep his credit clean and build again—a sweet deal.

It's easy to see why building apartments made sense to Jake. His only costs were the original $2,000 for the land and a few more dollars in architectural design. After that the big construction loan carried him. If a buyer put down enough cash to pay off the landowner's original $8,000, or just assume the mortgage, Jake would be home free. Even if he couldn't sell, Jake could just go into foreclosure and let the lender take the property back. He'd still have his profit, and he could always go into some other kind of work.

Most builders, of course, were not as unscrupulous as Jake, but enough were that a lot more apartment buildings were constructed than the market warranted. Jake is ancient history today. But he provides the contrast we need to understand the market's subsequent operation.

The Last Bull Market in Apartment Buildings

The last big building surge and oversupply of apartment units occurred during and immediately after the recession of 1975. Those days, however, already were quite different than the fifties and sixties. Landowners no longer offered subordinated seconds—when a builder lost the property to foreclosure, original landowners who couldn't handle taking over the first lost their money—they wanted cash. Lenders checked builders' estimates very closely for evidence of padding. Builders no longer could make a profit on the construction alone. Now they had to sell to make money.

Jake was still in the apartment-building market. By then, rents were about $250 a month; so a ten-unit building had a monthly potential of $2,500. The price of the building might be $200,000, and payments on an eight percent loan were about $1,500. That still left $1,000 for taxes, maintenance, insurance, and so forth. As long as vacancies weren't too high, an owner might have a *postive cash flow* of $300 to $500 a month on such a building!

In 1975, of course, land was still available, though not as cheaply as before, and construction loans were available, though at higher interest and under more scrutiny. Putting up $25,000 in cash for the land, Jake built again, hoping to find a buyer. But after the 1975 recession, there was an oversupply of apartment buildings from Florida to California. Again months of free rent were offered to tenants; again rents went down. Jake couldn't sell. His construction loan—which was for a term of only eighteen months—came due, and Jake couldn't get permanent financing to pay if off. He was forced into foreclosure, and this time, Jake stopped building.

In the late 1970s, many builders were in similar predica-
ments, and they, too, stopped building. It just didn't make
sense anymore. But when construction slowed, what started
as an oversupply quickly became a shortage. Suddenly, there
were too few apartments. Instead of offering a free month's
rent to move in, owners started raising rents. It was a boom
market all over again. Toward the beginning of the 1980s, Jake
considered going back into apartment construction, but he
realized that it wasn't possible to make a profit. Let's see why.

Today's Market

As mentioned, when the oversupply of the mid-1970s turned
into a shortage in the late 1970s, apartment-house owners
started raising rents dramatically. Raising rents, as we have
seen, has a multiplying effect on price. Let's take an example:
What is the price of an apartment building with ten units,
where each unit rents for $100 a month? If we assume a gross
income multiplier (GIM) of 8, we find the price by first calculating the monthly income:

$$
\begin{array}{rl}
\$ \quad 100 & \text{unit rent} \\
\times \quad 10 & \text{units} \\
\hline
\$ \ 1,000 & \text{monthly income}
\end{array}
$$

Then the annual income is:

$$
\begin{array}{rl}
\$ \ 1,000 & \\
\times \quad 12 & \text{months} \\
\hline
\$12,000 & \text{annual income}
\end{array}
$$

Then the price, using the multiplier of 8 is:

$$
\begin{array}{rl}
\$12,000 & \\
\times \quad 8 & \text{multiplier} \\
\hline
\$96,000 &
\end{array}
$$

The building is worth $96,000. But what happens to the price
when the owner raises rents by only $25? That's not an enor-
mous increase, even though it is 25% of the previous rent.

$$
\begin{array}{rl}
\$\quad 125 & \text{unit rent} \\
\times \quad\quad 10 & \text{units} \\
\hline
\$\quad 1{,}250 & \text{monthly income} \\
\times \quad\quad 12 & \\
\hline
\$\ 15{,}000 & \text{annual income} \\
\times \quad\quad\quad 8 & \text{multiplier} \\
\hline
\$120{,}000 & \text{new price for building}
\end{array}
$$

By raising the rent only $25 a month, the owner suddenly has increased the value of his building by $24,000.

With the shortage in apartments causing rents to shoot up, investors saw the potential for quick profits and moved immediately into the apartment-building market. The result was a dramatic increase in the demand for apartment buildings at the same time the demand for single-family housing was rising. The price of *all* housing rose sharply.

In apartment buildings, the multipliers used changed suddenly from the 6–8 range to the 10–12 range. To go back to our example, if a multiplier of 12 is used on an annual income of $15,000, we see a striking result.

$$
\begin{array}{rl}
\$\ 15{,}000 & \text{annual income} \\
\times \quad\quad 12 & \text{multiplier} \\
\hline
\$180{,}000 &
\end{array}
$$

Suddenly, *without raising rents,* the building has taken another jump in value—this time by $60,000! Needless to say, in the late 1970s, everyone wanted apartment buildings. But what did this mean for people like Jake who wanted to build them?

Jake found that landowners, who saw what houses and apartment buildings were bringing, quickly jacked up their land prices. At the same time, the general inflation sent building costs soaring—with land, a 10-unit building, Jake discovered, would cost something like $180,000 to build. If people were buying, of course, it made sense to build. Or did it? Jake looked at rents. At $125 a month per unit, he only could count on $1,250 a month from the 10-unit building. But a loan for $150,000 at 12 percent interest would make his payments $1,542 a month. Adding another $650 for taxes, insurance and other costs, his monthly expenses would be about $2,200. The property would show a *cash loss* of nearly $1,000 a month.

Who would make such an investment? Jake wondered. He knew that the current speculative fever in apartment buildings was causing buyers to purchase with the hope of increased prices in the future. But what if the fever cooled by the time Jake got his buildings up? Could he sell them then? Like many other builders, Jake decided not to get into the market, and the shortage of rental apartments continues.

Jake had discovered the *discrepancy between rental rates and price*. Apartment rentals today simply don't justify the price of the building—it can be justified only if it remains the same while rental rates climb higher. At some point the piper must be paid—the upward speculation in prices has to respond to the reality of rents.

Rumors of price collapse occurred in the recession of 1981–1982. There were whispers that the prices of apartment buildings wouldn't continue to rise forever. That was all it took—just the rumor—to make people hesitate in their purchases, and the market suddenly went flat. Those who had bought at multipliers of 12 and 14 found themselves with huge negative cash flows, even after consideration for tax shelters. What could they do? Some converted for profit into condominiums, while many others simply held on, hoping that rents would rise eventually. That was the critical element—rents. In our last example, rents for a 10-unit apartment building were only $1,250 a month; yet expenses were about $2,200. If rents rose to $220 a month per unit, then income and expense would be in balance. Owners could easily afford to keep the property and even have some hope of selling. For owners who held on, the question became: How soon will rents rise?

LIMITS ON RENT INCREASES: INCOME

There are two major factors that keep rents from rising—one natural, the other artificial—each highly significant in the apartment-rental market of the 1980s. The first limitation is *income*.

As we noted earlier, owning a home is part of the American dream. It's part of what young people expect out of American life—they'll grow up, get married, have kids, and own a home. That's certainly not everyone's dream, but it is the goal of a vast number of Americans. Those Americans who can afford to, as a rule, buy the homes they live in. That means that most of the people who live in apartments are those who can't afford to buy a home. Apartment dwellers, for the most part, tend to be either young or elderly.

Elderly Tenants

The elderly—who have sold their homes and want a smaller place to live, or who simply cannot afford to live elsewhere because of fixed or otherwise limited incomes—make excellent tenants. They cannot, however, afford to pay high rents. Even a modest yearly increase of ten percent is often sufficient to force them out.

Hazel is just such a person. She lives in a one-bedroom apartment in Santa Monica, California. Her rent—which does not include electricity, gas or garbage, but does include water—is $325 a month. Her total monthly income is about $600, including social security and a small pension from her deceased husband. That leaves Hazel with only $275 a month for utilities, food, transportation, entertainment, and medical expenses not covered by Medicare. It's obvious that she cannot afford to pay more rent. When rent increases are spoken of, Hazel raises her fist and calls landlords "Vultures!"

In fact, Hazel cannot really afford $325 a month. But she wants to live in a good, well-lighted building, in an area of the city where she feels safe. So each month she scrapes together enough money to pay the rent. Unbeknown to Hazel, however, the owner of her apartment building has just sold. There are five units in the building, with a total monthly rent of $1,625 and an annual rental income of $19,500. The buyer purchased at a price of $234,000 (the GIM was 12).

New Owner's Cost

$	325	unit income
×	5	number of units
$	1,625	total monthly income
×	12	annualized
$	19,500	total annual income
×	12	multiplier
$234,000		price

The new buyer put $50,000 down, which left her with a loan of about $184,000. The payments on the loan at 14% interest came to about $2,200 a month. There were also other costs:

Monthly Expenses on Hazel's Apartment Building

principal and interest on mortgage	$2,200
taxes	225
insurance	50
maintenance	150
water	60
miscellaneous	50
total monthly costs	$2,735
income monthly	1,625
negative cash flow (loss)	($1,110) monthly

The new owner was faced with raising more than $1,100 a month just to keep the building financially solvent. In her high tax bracket, of course, she could write off some of the loss. Despite the tax shelter, however, she still had a considerable negative cash flow. Raising rents seemed the only solution. So, a month after the apartment building was sold, Hazel received a form letter from the new owner. She read it with trembling hands.

Dear Tenant:

Allow me to introduce myself. I'm the new owner of Westview Apartments. I intend to keep our building in good shape, and sometime next year I'll have each unit repainted on the inside. I'm sure you'll agree it's long overdue, and that painting will make your unit more pleasant.

I also want to mention something not quite as pleasant, but necessary. As you know, costs of everything from soup to nuts are rising. The former owner indicates that there has not been a rent increase in the past six months. As the new owner, I was only able to purchase the building on the assumption that I could increase rents to match increased costs (taxes, insurance, mortgage payments, etc.). Therefore, I hope you'll understand that I must raise the rent by 10 percent, effective in two months. This is an increase of $32.50 per month. I'm sure you'll see that the increase is far less than this year's cost of living increase, as shown by the consumer price index.

If you have any questions, please feel free to write or call me. I feel you are an excellent tenant and hope you'll be able to keep living in my building.

Hazel tore the letter into tiny pieces.

The new owner's rent increase would bring in only an additional $160 a month, which would reduce her negative cash flow to about $950 a month. The owner realized that she'd have to raise rents every six months for three years before rental income matched expenses. To her, $32.50 seemed a tiny increase, especially considering the amount she needed to balance her books.

Hazel, on the other hand, saw the new rent increase as catastrophic. Her income had not recently increased, although it probably would, since social security is pegged to rises in consumer prices. The $32.50 amounted to 12 percent of the $275 she had to spend. If she paid the new rent, her monthly income available for food and all her other expenses would be reduced to $242.50.

The burden was simply too much for Hazel. She simply didn't have the income to stay where she was. Reluctantly, Hazel moved out and found a cheaper apartment in a less desirable part of town.

The new owner regretted seeing Hazel go, but she had her own problems. She put the apartment up for rent, and it was taken immediately by the Smiths, a young, recently married couple—part of the second major group of renters in the country.

Young Couples as Tenants

The Smiths had been married only six months, and, for the moment, a one-bedroom apartment seemed ideal to them. Since they both worked, they could afford $360 a month for rent.

While it might seem that Hazel was left out in the cold so that the new owner's problems could be solved, that's not really the case. Remember, the new owner won't be satisfied until rents rise enough to at least meet expenses, which only makes sense. She wants to get $2,200 a month out of the five rentals, or $440 apiece. The price will rise quickly to that point, and when it does, it will have a dramatic effect on the price of the building.

New value of property	
unit rental	$ 440
total monthly income	2,200
annualized	26,400
multiplier	× 12
new building value	$316,800

Seeing the potential profit to be made—bought at $234,000 and sold at $316,800, yielding over $80,000—the new owner will undoubtedly be tempted to sell. If she does, the next owner suddenly will find a similar situation prevailing. At $316,800, rents will need to total $3,500 a month, or $700 per unit, before income matches expenses (new mortgage payment, taxes, insurance, etc.). So rents will continue to rise.

Along the way, our new couple will begin to feel the rent pinch, and they'll begin to say, "Let's move to something cheaper," or, "Let's make these payments toward a house of our own. Then, at least, some of our money will come back in equity."

Eventually, the current owner, or a future one, will reach the point where it's impossible to rent the units out to anyone for the money desired. Potential tenants who want to rent but don't have the money will be excluded, and those who do have the money will prefer to buy.

In the United States, the income of potential tenants is simply not rising fast enough to keep pace with the rental rates required to justify the constantly higher prices of apartment buildings. As long as the income of prospective tenants remains low, apartment-building owners are restricted in the rents they can charge. The demand for apartments is certainly there, but people can't rent if they don't have the money, and their limited income keeps rental rates down.

LIMITS ON RENT INCREASES: RENT CONTROL

There is another factor in keeping rental rates low, one with far more serious implications for apartment-building owners— *rent control*.

Remember Hazel, the elderly tenant left out in the cold when her income didn't rise with her rent? There are a lot of Hazels in America, and their voices and needs are being heard. In city after city, concerned public officials are trying to determine what to do with Hazel and others with her plight. They want Hazel to be able to afford housing, but they don't want to pay for it through government aid. Rent control is the quickest and easiest solution they can find.

From Los Angeles to New York to Florida, communities are enacting some form of rent control. The control typically involves restricting the size and frequency of rent increases that landlords can make on buildings. There are also some exemptions to the laws, so that single-family homes, for example, are exempted.

Hazel Under Rent Control

If Hazel had been in a rent-control area when her new landlady tried to raise the rent, things might have gone much differently. Depending on the conditions of the rent-control act in effect, had Hazel complained to the rent-control board, the owner may have been told that:

1.) Rents cannot be raised except once in twelve months. Since rents were raised six months earlier, it will be another six months before a raise can be made.

2.) A rental increase must be based on actual increases in the owner's costs of operation. Such costs include increased taxes, insurance, maintenance, utilities, and so forth. Increases in mortgage payments are not considered.

3.) In any event, no increase beyond 7 percent per year is allowed.

(*Note to reader:* These conditions are a combination of those imposed by several cities.)

Hazel's rent raise would have been postponed for six months. In addition, the raise would reflect only the owner's actual increased costs, and, in any event, could be no more than 7 percent, or about $25 a month. Since Hazel had a social security increase coming soon, she might have been able to handle the rent increase.

Rent Control and Apartment Owners

Rent control is good for Hazel, but what about the apartment-building owner? With rent control, she's pulling her hair out. She bought the building at an inflated gross income multiplier. Now it will be years, perhaps even decades, before rent increases catch up with her payments.

As a result of the rent-control ruling, this new owner probably won't be able to sell the building to someone else. Since there's little or no appreciation to be made in the future, the property will simply become unsalable. Our new owner will rue the day she bought the apartment building, and she may seriously consider just letting it go in foreclosure. Or, she may begin thinking about conversion to condominiums. What was good for Hazel in the short term, may not work out so well in the long run.

The two limitations on raising rents—the slowness of personal income increases and the passage of restrictive rent-control laws—have put a lid on the apartment-building market in many areas of the country.

New Construction in a Limited-Income/Rent-Control Market

But, what of Jake, our apartment-building developer? What will rent control do to Jake? Although we haven't mentioned it, rent-control ordinances rarely restrict the chargeable rent on *new* apartment buildings. In theory, Jake could build an apartment structure and charge anything he liked, at least initially.

Jake investigated buildings in Hazel's area and found several problems. The cost of suitable land for apartment building was very high in the area, another example of the fact that good, close-in land is used up in the majority of U.S. cities. Further, inflation has pushed the cost of building materials up by leaps and bounds every year.

Jake calculated that it would cost him close to $30,000 to build each unit of a five-unit apartment building. When he added in another $100,000 for land cost, the total price of the structure came to about $250,000.

$$
\begin{array}{r}
\$\ 30,000 \quad \text{per unit} \\
\times \qquad 5 \\
\hline
\$150,000 \\
+\ 100,000 \quad \text{land cost} \\
\hline
\$250,000
\end{array}
$$

This, of course, was before loan costs and profit. When Jake added in $25,000 in interest charges (on a mortgage used to construct the building and help finance the land) and another $25,000 in profit, he found that he'd have to sell the building for $300,000. That would mean renting the units out for close to $700 a month.

Jake reasoned that he couldn't fill the building if rents were that high, at least not then. Currently, the most he could rent the units out for was $500 a month, and after the building was six months old, it fell under rent-control restrictions. Overall, it looked like it would be very hard to sell his new apartment building, so Jake did what made most sense. He didn't build at all.

With fewer new apartment buildings further restricting the supply, the demand for existing structures increases. Ultimately, this should result in higher rents. As we've seen, however, low personal income puts a natural restraint on rent increases, while rent controls put an artificial restraint on them.

THE FUTURE FOR APARTMENT BUILDINGS

Overall, during the early to mid-1980s, *apartment buildings don't offer the opportunity that was promised just a few years earlier.*

There are, of course, exceptions. Forced sales—where the building's owner simply cannot continue with negative cash flow—may be an opportunity. Banks maintain an "REO" (real estate owned) department, in which they manage and try to resell property they've reclaimed in foreclosure. On such property, banks often are willing to give a below-market-rate mortgage to an investor who will relieve them of the management headache.

Additionally, in certain areas of the country—some parts of Texas (particularly around Houston), the Ft. Lauderdale-St. Petersburg area in Florida, parts of Oregon and the Pacific Northwest, and a few areas in the Midwest (but not Minnesota)—high multipliers simply did not occur. In these places, cheap land, cheap labor, and limited demand acted in concert to keep the market low. Because the prices of apartment buildings never soared, when the national market collapsed these buildings had nowhere to fall. Even today in these areas, it may still be possible to buy an apartment building with a multiplier of under 10 and either break even or have a positive cash flow.

These are excellent investments that are simply a matter of coming up with the down payment and then letting the building cover itself. Eventually prices will rise (caused by the incessant demand of today's housing shortage), and these buildings can be sold for a profit.

I suggest that investors *do not* buy any apartment buildings with an *after-tax, negative cash flow.* Further, only those investors with a strong and continuing income should consider apartment buildings with any negative cash flow at all. For most of us that means *staying away from apartment-building investments, unless the building can show a positive cash flow.*

Chapter Eight

THE FUTURE FOR
MOBILE HOME PARKS

In 1975, in *How to Buy and Sell Real Estate for Financial Security* (McGraw-Hill), I suggested that mobile home parks were the strongest possible real estate investment. And, of the many ways to make money in real estate during the last few years, some of the more impressive profits have indeed come from mobile home parks. While the era of enormous profits from this type of investment may now be behind us, at least temporarily, mobile home parks remain a solid real estate investment.

WHAT IS A MOBILE HOME PARK?

A mobile home park, essentially, is land upon which pads have been built or areas set aside for mobile homes. The park usually has a single owner/investor who rents out individual pads, which are provided with utilities—such as water, electricity, gas and sewer. Often there are streets connecting the pads and, in some cases, central lawn areas, swimming pools, recreation halls and other amenities.

There are at least three types of parks: *mom and pop parks,*
with the owner living in one of the homes or nearby, usually
have about twenty pads; *modern parks* are much larger, often
adults-only, communities with many amenities; and *recreational
parks* have pads for more-permanent mobile homes as well as
some for recreational vehicles and trailers. (We'll go into this
last group in the chapter on vacation property.) Let's look at
how the market for mobile home parks has changed in the past
few years.

BIG BUCKS IN MOBILE HOME PARKS

In the mid-1970s Dick decided he wanted to invest in real
estate. After looking at homes, he realized he didn't want to
sit on his investment for several years before selling it for a
profit. He wanted something where he could see his money
grow, something more active than a house; so he investigated
mobile home parks. He quickly discovered that he couldn't
afford any of the large parks available. He learned that mobile
home parks, like other investment properties, are evaluated on
the basis of the income they produce. For example, in a typical
mobile home park with 100 units, where each pad is rented for
$100, the approximate price (assuming a multiplier of 10) would
be $1,200,000.

$	100	per unit
×	100	units
$	10,000	total monthly income
×	12	months
$	120,000	gross annual income
×	10	multiplier
$1,200,000		price

Since it was possible to get 80 percent financing on mobile
home parks, in order to buy this park, Dick would have to raise
20% of $1.2 million, or $240,000. That was $200,000 more than
he had. (As we'll see later on, financing *new* mobile home parks
is a big stumbling block in the market, but it's not so difficult

for existing parks.) But Dick persisted until he found a "mom and pop" park that had 25 units, each renting for $35. With a multiplier of 12, the price would be about $125,000.

$$
\begin{array}{rl}
\$\quad 35 & \text{per unit} \\
\times \quad 25 & \text{units} \\
\hline
\$\quad 875 & \text{total monthly income} \\
\times \quad 12 & \text{months} \\
\hline
\$\ 10,500 & \text{gross annual income} \\
\times \quad 12 & \text{multiplier} \\
\hline
\$126,000 & \text{price}
\end{array}
$$

The sleepy atmosphere of the little park reminded Dick of "trailer" parks of the 1940s and 1950s that he'd seen in the movies. It was obvious why it charged so much less for its space than the big modern park. The small park had no swimming pool or recreation hall, no spacious lawns or flowered drives—all amenities available in the larger park.

"No Vacancy" Means There's a Need Waiting to Be Filled

But Dick had done some homework, and he wondered if he could somehow justify modernization and rent increases in this park. In looking at other parks he'd seen very few empty pads. And he learned that even in the mom and pop parks (rapidly purchased by investors in the mid-1970s), prices for pads were being raised far higher than $35 a month after relatively minor cosmetic work on the parks. Dick knew an opportunity when he saw it—he bought the park.

Putting 80% down on this older park would still leave Dick with some of his initial capital of $40,000.

$$
\begin{array}{rl}
\$125,000 & \text{price} \\
\times \quad 80\% & \\
\hline
\$100,000 & \text{loan} \\
\$\ 25,000 & \text{down payment}
\end{array}
$$

Dick used his remaining $15,000, and some moie that he borrowed, to upgrade the park. He widened some roads, put in a small recreation room and a spa, . . . and doubled the rents. Many of the tenants were shocked at the rent increases, which they felt were totally unjustified. They pointed out that the cost of living had not doubled overnight, nor had the expenses of owning the park. What right did Dick have to suddenly double the rent?

Dick hadn't expected quite so much flak. He figured that most of the tenants understood that $35 a month was ridiculously cheap, and that they wouldn't be surprised if a new owner raised the rents to more competitive rates. What he didn't realize was that many of the tenants depended on the artificially low rent to maintain their standard of living. By keeping rents low, the former owners had encouraged these tenants to stay.

Dick sympathized with their plight and agreed to phase in the rent increases over a period of time. But that was the best he would do. Most of the tenants approved of the improvements Dick had made and eventually accepted the increase. Seven out of the twenty-five, however, hooked up their trailers and moved. When Dick found his park was nearly one-third empty, he didn't panic. He realized that the vacancies presented a new opportunity.

Turning a Problem into a Challenge

Dick borrowed more money and improved the pads. After relocating some tenants, he made five new pads from the seven that were empty, each large enough to accommodate the new double-wide homes that were so popular. (A single mobile home is about 12 feet wide; a double-wide home consists of two singles, designed at the factory to be assembled together on the site. A decade ago, singles were virtually the only mobile homes available. Today, however, double- and even triple-wides are the rule.) Around his five new pads, Dick planted shrubs, put in fences for privacy, and then offered them for rent at $85 a space. They all rented within a few months.

Dick put to use what he had learned upon visiting mobile home manufacturers. He had seen how the homes were built, what was available, and how much they cost. More importantly, he learned that the major complaint of mobile home manufacturers and dealers was the lack of pads to accommodate the new, wider homes they were building. New parks were going up much slower than new homes were being built, and the demand for parks large enough to accommodate the new homes was simply enormous. In Dick's area, space for a double-wide home was rented almost overnight.

Dick arranged his five pads in a "wing" of his mobile home park, a new modern wing, and anticipated converting the remaining pads for double-wides as soon as the older tenants moved out. (Not all older parks can be converted in this manner, but Dick's original pads were already quite large. In many older parks, only singles can ever be accommodated, and rent increases in these parks have been more moderate.)

Dick's income from his park, after all his rent increases took effect, was $1,685.

$$
\begin{array}{r}
\$\ \ 70 \text{ per unit} \\
\times \quad 18 \text{ pads} \\
\hline
\$1,260
\end{array}
$$

plus

$$
\begin{array}{rr}
85 \text{ per unit} & \\
\times \quad \ \ 5 \text{ pads} & \$\ \ 1,260 \\
\hline
\$\ \ 425 & +\quad 425 \\
& \hline
& \$\ \ 1,685 \text{ income} \\
& \times \quad \ \ 12 \text{ months (annualized)} \\
& \hline
& \$\ 20,220 \\
& \times \quad \ \ 12 \text{ multiplier} \\
& \hline
& \$242,640
\end{array}
$$

With his rent raises and conversions, Dick had increased the value of his mobile home park by more than $100,000.

$$
\begin{array}{lr}
\text{new value} & \$242,640 \\
\text{purchase price} & \underline{125,000} \\
& \$117,640 \quad \text{increase in equity}
\end{array}
$$

Dick was able to accomplish this because he moved into a market with a burgeoning demand and a very limited supply. When Dick raised the rents, most of his older tenants couldn't find anywhere else to move; so whether they felt they could afford to or not, they remained.

Does Modernization Cost More than It's Worth?

Careful readers may be wondering, at this point, about Dick's upgrading. It would seem that his efforts actually lost him money!

Before Conversion		After Conversion
$ 70	rent	$ 85
× 7	pads	× 5
$490		$425

By upgrading he changed a potential income of $490 from seven pads into an income of $425 from five pads. After upgrading, Dick's income was $65 per month less than it would have been had he not made the improvements. But Dick was looking to the future. He felt that it would be difficult to further increase the rent on the *older* units in his park; he had reached the upper limits of those tenants' ability to pay.

On the other hand, the new tenants with the modern homes usually had higher incomes or greater capital resources. Dick reasoned that rents could be raised on the new units more frequently and at higher levels than on the older units. Indeed, within a year the newer modern parks were charging $125 a month for double-wide spaces, and Dick, whose park offered fewer amenities, had raised his rents up to $115. At the same time, he had only been able to increase the rents on the older units to $80 per month.

Without Conversion		One Year After Conversion
$ 80	rent	$115
× 7	pads	× 5
$560		$575

Profit Multiplying from Rent Increases

Two things should be obvious: first, in the 1970s, with little or no rent control, the market in mobile home parks was such that quick rent increases were possible; secondly, the value of a mobile home park increased with each rent raise. We can pinpoint the relationship between the appreciation and rent increases. If Dick, for example, raised his rents only $1 a month on his 23 units, what effect would that have on the value of his park?

$	1	per month increase
×	23	units
$	23	monthly total increase
×	12	months
$	276	gross annual income increase
×	12	multiplier
$3,312		price appreciation

Because of this income-price relationship, simply raising monthly rents by $1 boosts the park's value by over $3,300! And because of the fierce demand for mobile home spaces in the 1970s, new owners readily increased rents, particularly those who bought older, mom and pop parks where rents had been kept low. I've seen parks where investors received a return on their money in excess of 100 percent a year—three and four years in a row! It's hard to argue with profits like that.

That's how Dick made his money. He moved into a market and converted an older product into a modern one, thereby benefiting from the modern price. But, of course, times change and so do markets, particularly the mobile home market.

MOBILE HOME PARKS TODAY

Today there are few mom and pop parks left anywhere in the country, and the prices of those which remain are almost impossibly steep. The idea of modernizing a small older park really isn't feasible anymore. In addition, many elderly people who once lived in these small parks have been displaced. Where do they find living space in a tight rental market?

Tenant Groups Fight Back

To respond to these problems, particularly in California and Florida, tenant coalitions have formed to fight displacement. They have pointed out, for example, that the term "mobile" home is a misnomer: most modern mobile homes rest on concrete foundations and consist of several units "sewn" together; they are connected to water, power and sewer, and frequently have air-conditioning units attached. Such a home is hardly mobile in the way that the old trailers were. It can take several days and cost several thousand dollars to prepare a modern mobile home for moving to a new setup. Tenant groups have argued that dramatic rent increases are a burden to mobile home owners, who, ironically, have less mobility than those who rent apartments.

The tenant groups, therefore, have worked diligently for local ordinances that restrict the owner's ability to have them displaced. In many areas, an owner now must give up to a full year's notice of intent to have a tenant moved, even if the reason is that the tenant refuses to pay a rent increase. Additionally, tenant groups have worked to restrict the amount of rent increases allowed, and, in some cases, owners are now prohibited from raising rents beyond a certain index, such as the consumer price index. (If the CPI rises 10 percent, then rents cannot be raised more than 10 percent.)

Such rules have slowed the pace of price growth in mobile home parks. Dick can no longer arbitrarily double the rent or make subsequent, significant raises, which slows the increase in value of his park. (It also prevents older tenants from being forced out because of their inability to pay.)

Park owners who bought just before the new restrictive laws went into effect—paying on the basis of a GIM of 12 to 14, and assuming their profits would come from subsequent rent raises—found themselves in a tough spot. They could not charge enough to meet current expenses, and, with slow rent increases, it would be many years before income equaled expenses. Buying existing mobile home parks, particularly when the owners persist in demanding high multipliers, has become an exceedingly risky business.

But two areas of opportunity remain in mobile home parks. The first is condominium conversion.

CONDOMINIUM CONVERSION IN A MOBILE HOME PARK

It is possible to convert a mobile home park to condominium ownership, but much more difficult than with an apartment building. The problem, as we've just seen, is that mobile home owners are not very mobile. When a park owner wants to convert to a condominium, these tenants may have neither the money to buy their rental spaces, nor the money to move.

As a result, many states and localities have restricted mobile home park conversion—in many cases several years' advance notice is required; in others, a positive vote by the tenant association is necessary; elsewhere, conversion is simply prohibited. But where conversion *is* allowed, the profit for the park owner is similar to that for the apartment-house owner who converts.

Combining Mobile Home Profits with Conversion Profits

Dick decided to convert his mobile home park to a condominium. It took him three years to do the necessary legal work, comply with local codes, and otherwise finish the project—but, it was worthwhile. Additional upgrading had left Dick with 20 pads, renting for an average of $100 per month; so before conversion, his park was worth $288,000.

$	100	per month, average rent
×	20	units
$	2,000	gross monthly income
$	24,000	annual income
×	12	multiplier
$288,000		park value

After Dick converted, he sold the spaces on which the homes were parked for $25,000 apiece.

$$\begin{array}{r} \$ \ 25,000 \quad \text{units} \\ \times \quad\quad 20 \\ \hline \$500,000 \end{array}$$

By converting to condos and selling, he virtually doubled the value of his capital.

And it wasn't such a bad thing for the mobile home owners. For just $25,000 they became property owners. And if they now had tax and mortgage payments, they no longer had to worry about rent increases. In the current market, of course, these figures will sound low. Today, a mobile home owner might pay anything from $200 to $600 a month in pad rental; and the price of the land under a mobile home may be as much as $150,000, or even more, depending on the location.

Converting Mobile Home Parks, Though Rarely Done, Makes Dollar Sense

Nevertheless, I feel that condo conversion is currently more realistic in a mobile home park (although done less often) than in an apartment building, for one reason—the absolute price. In an apartment building, a tenant who has been paying $500 a month rent, for example, can hardly be expected to buy the unit when it's suddenly offered for sale at, say, $125,000. With a normal down payment of 20 percent and interest rates between 12 and 14 percent, the monthly payments on such a unit would be about $1,200 to $1,400. Few tenants, these days, can handle monthly payments nearly three times as much as their rent.

For the mobile home owner, however, who has been renting his pad for $250 a month and is suddenly faced with the impending sale for, say, $35,000, the burden is not nearly so great. With the same interest rates and a normal down payment ($7,000 here, as opposed to $25,000 for the apartment condo), monthly payments will only be about $350. Despite the increase in monthly payments, the absolute amount ($350) may well be affordable. The absolute amount may be far higher, of course, depending on the park. But since the tenant has already paid for the mobile home, the additional expense for the land is not such a burden.

It should be noted that many mobile home owners, especially the elderly, pay cash or carry a relatively small mortgage on the home. Typically, such people take the money out of their conventional home and pay off a mobile home, thereby hoping to avoid monthly payments in retirement. While the financial burden of a condo conversion is naturally greater for these people than for others, many such retired families have sufficient resources to make the required down payment. In most cases, the *combined* cost of the land and the unit is close to *half* that for conventional housing.

The point about absolute costs in mobile homes cannot be overemphasized. The park owner can charge a relatively low price because he or she is selling only the land and such improvements as streets, utilities, landscaping, and additional amenities.

Now let's move on to the second area of opportunity for investors in mobile home parks—building new parks.

BUILDING A NEW PARK—PROFIT VERSUS HARDSHIP

Because it is manufactured in a plant, a mobile home may cost as little as one-third to one-half the price of a comparable, conventional home. The benefits of assembly-line production, which make automobile construction relatively cheap, also apply to mobile homes. In the United States, the mobile home industry annually turns out hundreds of thousands of homes on assembly lines, frequently producing an entire house in two days or less! Acceptance of manufactured homes, however, has been slow in coming in this country. (This contrasts with other countries, such as Russia, where nearly *all* homes are plant manufactured.) But as new techniques allow mobile homes to look more conventional, it's likely that their acceptance will increase dramatically.

Lower Cost of Parks

What has the low absolute cost of the mobile home to do with the investor, who is usually more interested in the real estate beneath it?

Drew heard about the profits in mobile home parks and decided to investigate. But, he was stymied. Owners of the few, available older parks wanted an "arm and a leg" for them. Drew was about ready to give up when he noticed an interesting thing. Although he couldn't find a park to buy at a reasonable price, the demand for park space was still enormous. As people found conventional housing increasingly expensive and overpriced, they began looking at mobile homes. The problem with mobile homes, however, was finding parks in which to put them.

Drew began investigating the possibility of building a mobile home park, reasoning that it should be very simple. After all, what was he building? Besides roads, utilities, fences and some landscaping, Drew would only need to build a clubhouse, a pool, and perhaps a tennis court. Unlike putting in an apartment building, Drew would avoid the biggest part of the expense—the building itself. By investing in a mobile home park, he'd have the advantages of an apartment building (rental income), without having to put up the structure.

And, with a *new* project, Drew could charge appropriate monthly rents—perhaps $500 to $600—even in most rent-controlled areas. With the heavy demand caused by the shortage of available space, such rent wouldn't be unreasonable if his park were especially nice and well located. Rent controls would prevent significant rent *increases*, but Drew was free to initially charge whatever the market allowed. So the question became: Would the rental income justify the cost of building, allowing for a profit? Drew made some quick calculations. If he built a 100-unit park and charged $500 a month in rent, his projected value was a phenomenal $6,000,000.

$$
\begin{array}{rl}
\$\quad 500 & \text{rent} \\
\times \quad 100 & \text{units} \\
\hline
\$\quad 50,000 & \text{monthly income}
\end{array}
$$

$$\begin{array}{r} \times \quad\quad 12 \\ \hline \$\ \ 600,000 \\ \times \quad\quad 10 \\ \hline \$6,000,000! \end{array}$$ gross annual income

multiplier*

(*A lower multiplier is used today.)

Drew didn't hesitate—he immediately began to look for a suitable piece of property.

Why Everyone Wants a Mobile Home Park . . . In Someone Else's City

Drew soon discovered an enormous problem: no one wanted a new mobile home park—not homeowners, not cities, not even lenders—it was an anathema. A mobile home park was something akin to the plague, it seemed, to just about everyone but the park owner and mobile home owners. What was it about mobile home parks that everyone hated? Drew found two problems which, though interrelated, affected two different groups.

Taxation

The first problem affected local communities and nearby homeowners sensitive to the way in which mobile homes traditionally have been taxed.

Although Drew realized that modern mobile homes aren't really mobile, he found that in most areas they were still treated as if they were. When a person bought a mobile home, he or she applied for a vehicle license, then paid a yearly fee to keep the license current. As with an automobile, it was assumed that the mobile home depreciates in value. Therefore, the licensing fee decreased each year. Mobile home buyers are often told by sellers of this advantage. Instead of paying the high property taxes common with conventional homes, they will pay comparatively low vehicle taxes. It's quite an incentive . . . for the mobile home buyer.

But it's just the opposite for the owners of conventional homes in areas surrounding a mobile home park. Through property taxes, homeowners pay for schools and libraries, street lighting and improvements, parks and community recreational facilities, police and fire protection, and all the other amenities that come from living in an established community. These people see mobile home owners as freeloaders who use the schools and libraries, benefit from fire and police protection, play in the parks, and so forth, without contributing to the burden of their cost.

It's easy to see why owners of conventional homes (through their elected representatives) are against local development of mobile home parks, and why Drew found it so hard to win approval for any land he considered suitable for the park he wished to build.

Of course, times are changing. Many states have awakened to the reality that mobile homes are mostly permanent and are beginning to tax them as traditional real estate, once they've been permanently placed on pads. Some communities now require that a *mobile* home have the capability to be moved from its site within a few hours. Since this is rarely possible for mobile homes placed on cement foundations, they are reclassified as conventional real estate and taxed accordingly. Unhappy with increased taxes, mobile home owners have frequently voiced their complaints. To the city and nearby homeowners, however, it is only right that mobile home owners share the tax burden. And when the tax burden is shared, there is far less resistance to the idea of building new parks.

Eventually, in a community where mobile homes were taxed as real property, Drew found a large lot near a residential area at the edge of town. Then, after months of wrangling with the city planning department, he got approval for a mobile home park. He didn't actually buy the property, however. Instead he put down a deposit on a sale contingent upon (1) zoning approval (which he now had) and (2) financing.

Securing Financing

Finding appropriate financing is the second big hurdle for those wanting to build mobile home parks. The problem arises from the nature of mobile home park occupancy.

The bank told Drew that before they'd issue him a permanent, 30-year loan, he would have to get a construction loan based on written estimates of the cost of building the park. He would have to hire a contractor and subcontractors, and then total the estimates submitted for the building, pool, spa, roads, pads, utility hookups, and any other amenities he planned. Then, assuming Drew owned the land free and clear (or could clear it somewhere along the way), a loan would be issued for the total estimate.

Drew estimated that it would cost $2,000,000 to build his park, in addition to land costs of $2,000,000. When he brought his loan package to the bank, the loan officer said that— assuming sufficient income from the future park to make the mortgage and all other payments (there was), and assuming that Drew was credit worthy (he was) and had a successful track record (he did)—they would consider making the loan.

The officer pointed out, however, that if the loan were approved it would have severe restrictions. No money would be paid, for example, until work was completed. Only after the roads were built would the bank issue a check to the construction company that built them. Additionally, no money would be released directly to Drew. This presented some problems, because some builders would not begin work without at least partial payment.

Drew began to see that working with a construction loan would be very difficult. But since he knew that his park would be worth about six million when completed, and that the land and building would cost only four million to buy and build, he decided to bear the difficulties. He applied for the loan.

The bank's loan committee turned him down.

Drew was astonished; he asked the loan officer if there had been some blemish on his application. Was there a bad credit report he didn't know about? And what about his experience?

She answered that none of these items really figured into the decision. Off the record, she said that the loan committee simply decided that the bank didn't want to make a construction loan on a mobile home park.

Drew was incredulous. "What's wrong with a mobile home park as an investment?"

"Nothing," she replied. "It's just a lousy subject for a construction loan." She explained that the bank normally only issued construction loans for a maximum of twelve months. There were no pay-back provisions on the loan during that period. The borrower simply had to pay back the full amount loaned, plus interest, at the end of the twelve-month period. "The way you do that," she continued, "is to get a 'take-out' or permanent loan, probably for thirty years, at the end of the 12-month period. Then you, or future buyers, make payments on this loan for the next thirty years, or until it's paid off."

Drew shook his head. He couldn't see what the problem was.

The loan officer smiled and said, "They just don't think you can do it all in only twelve months." Drew asked what she meant. To him it was perfectly obvious that he could build roads, buildings, pool, spa, and so forth in only four months. "One of the reasons for obtaining a permanent loan," she explained, "at least from our bank and probably from anyone else, is that you must first rent 70 percent of the park. The loan committee felt that you couldn't both build the park and rent 70 percent of it in twelve months."

Drew was beginning to understand. He'd been told by other park owners that the most difficult time for a new park was between the date of completion and the date it was filled. The problem was that future tenants had to find his park and decide to rent; then they had to have a mobile home built and moved to his park. There were real logistical problems. Unlike selling conventional homes, where the product was right there, here Drew essentially would be selling space. He'd have to coordinate his rentals with someone else's purchase of a mobile home, which would probably depend on the sale of their current home, as well as their ability to arrange financing.

"The loan committee," the officer continued, "checked back on past loans it had made on mobile home parks and found many foreclosures, because it took builders upwards of two years to get their parks 70 percent occupied. I'm sorry."

Drew left without the loan.

Fortunately, financing today is not nearly as difficult as when Drew applied. Seeing the profits available to builders, some lenders have extended their construction-loan periods up to two years. Further, many mobile home manufacturers will help a developer by putting units on the pads as soon as the park is completed. Then, when prospective tenants come by to look, they can literally buy a house already in place. I've seen arrangements such as this fill parks in as few as six months. A great deal, of course, depends on the area . . . and luck.

Eventually, Drew was able to arrange financing on the basis of such an arrangement with a manufacturer. He built his park and sold within a year for a handsome profit. To those who asked, Drew pointed out that little money could be made by owning and operating a mobile home park, unless you bought it years earlier when prices were lower. The profit, for him, came from building and selling.

Although it's not easy in today's market, the opportunity to make big money in mobile home parks remains strong. The need for homes, particularly inexpensive homes, is stronger today in America than ever before. And because mobile homes are probably the cheapest available answer, the demand for parks and park space should continue to boom. Whether it's finding a small, old park to modernize or building a big new park, the rewards are great for those with the fortitude and creativity to move ahead.

Mobile homes are a challenge waiting to be answered—a field with almost unlimited demand; buyers who can actually afford the homes; and lots of land suitable for development (or already developed), once the taxation and prejudice hurdles are overcome. What more can an investor ask for?

Chapter Nine

INVESTING IN SHOPPING CENTERS

"Invest in a shopping center? Who me? I haven't got that kind of money!" It's "common knowledge" that shopping centers cost millions of dollars. Buying one, or investing in one, is hopelessly beyond the means of the small to moderate investor. Or is it?

It's certainly true that a regional shopping center (with one or two major department stores and covering forty acres or more) or a super-regional center (with three or four major department stores and covering 100 acres or more) involve big bucks, and we'll reserve our discussion of these until the end of the chapter.

But there are other kinds of shopping centers which the small to moderate investor can get into, sometimes with only a few thousand dollars! These are what I call "bargain centers," not because of the kind of stores they have, but because of the small investment required. Before we get to the bargains, however, it's important to understand just what we mean by a "shopping center."

I recall hearing stories in my youth of the fabulous prices of commercial property in New York City. My father, who was a real estate broker, spoke with awe of deals involving prices as high as $5,000 a "front foot." "Imagine that," he'd say. "Someone was willing to pay $5,000 a foot to build a store on that street. Can you imagine what kind of business he'll have to do in order to justify that price?"

My father was touching on two concepts. First, the price paid for commercial property must be justified by the income the business received. In other words, you don't pay $5,000 a front foot to put up a lemonade stand. You need the kind of store that will bring in a lot of money. This still holds true today.

The second concept was that commercial property was sold on the basis of "front feet." Quite simply, the business buyer paid for street exposure. It didn't matter much if the store were 50 or 500 feet deep. It was exposure to the street, to people walking past, that counted. Except for some downtown urban areas, this concept of the "front foot" evaluation is as dead today as the twenty-cent gallon of gasoline. Understanding what happened to the "front foot" method of evaluating commercial property leads us right into shopping centers. Let's go back thirty-five years to the era just after the Second World War. Where were shops built in those days?

Then, as now, stores were built where the people were, and most of the people were in the city. When they shopped they went deeper into the city, to the center of shopping where all the big stores were located. These were such department stores as Macys, Gimbles, May Co. and Hales. Smaller merchants surrounded these larger stores. It was the spot to buy whatever you wanted.

From the merchants' point of view, it was something like fishing. The store faced a city street flowing with business people on their way to work, vagrants with nothing to do, tourists, and some potential customers. The trick was to hook those potential customers, so they would see the store, come in and buy. The hook was the *storefront*, which usually meant lots of glass with bright bold displays of the merchandise inside. The best store was the one with the biggest hook, or the most frontage. The ideal store had fifty feet of street frontage, even if it were only ten feet deep. The worst store was the one with only ten feet in frontage, though it might be fifty feet deep. With such little frontage, the potential customer was likely to pass right by before even realizing that the store was there. No wonder property sold on the basis of the front foot. The critical factor in these older, downtown shopping areas was that people *walked* to these stores. Some lived or worked nearby. Others took the train or bus into town, and a few drove and parked in outlying parking lots.

Beginning in the 1950s, things changed. Growing numbers of cars carried people to homes in the suburbs. The central city, where the big stores were located, was difficult to get to and impossible to park near—it was no longer convenient to shop downtown. So enterprising individuals said to themselves, "If we're having trouble getting the shoppers to the stores, why not bring the stores to the shoppers?" They did just that.

Small "shopping centers"—a drugstore, a food market, a novelty store, and perhaps a small clothier—began springing up in the suburbs. They served some of the needs of the immediate community, but not all. Larger centers were needed. Probably the first, major, regional shopping center was located in Minneapolis. It covered hundreds of acres, was enclosed, and was totally surrounded by parking areas. It was a new concept—a shopping center linked to the automobile. The idea, as we all know, was to drive to the center, leave your car, and walk in; once inside, you were in a controlled environment, warm in the winter and cool in the summer.

For the merchant it was a dream come true. Instead of fighting it out for the fish on a commercial street, now he or she was inside. Most important, people came to the shopping center with the express purpose of buying. *All* the people in the center were potential customers.

This is not to say that the storefront wasn't an important lure; it certainly was. But equally important was having a store large enough to accommodate the many wares a merchant wanted to sell. Total area (as well as location within the center) assumed new importance, resulting in a new concept for retail sales—the *square* foot. The new shopping center property was sold to the developer on the basis of square feet instead of street frontage. (In fact, the center often had no frontage at all in the old sense. Rather, it butted up against major arteries

onto which the developer provided vehicle entrances and exits.)
And inside the shopping center, individual stores were leased
on the basis of square feet, not front feet. For the last twenty
years, nearly all shopping centers have adopted the square-
foot basis of calculating value.

"STRIP" SHOPPING CENTERS

I'm sure many readers are saying to themselves, "So what if
it's a front foot or a square foot. What's the difference if I can't
afford it?"

Ernie, a small investor, found out that it makes a lot of difference. Ernie had lived in Los Angeles all his life, and if there
was anything he knew to be true about the city, it was that it
was totally geared to automobiles—there were more miles of
pavement in Los Angeles than the total area of some of
America's other major cities. It's become a well-known joke
that, in Los Angeles, people even drive to the mailbox. The
image is that nobody, but nobody, walks anywhere.

Los Angeles—where drive-in restaurants had their heydays,
and where gas stations reigned supreme—adjusted to the
image. So it was not unusual to find two or three gas stations
at an intersection, with another set just a few blocks away.
After all, those millions of cars had to have fuel. The major oil
companies competed furiously with each other for a piece of
the L.A. action.

Then came the oil crunch, inflation, and gas shortages.
Then, when gas was plentiful once again, the price soared.
Suddenly, in the land of big engines and shining chrome,
people began driving less and conserving more. Thousands of
gas stations weren't needed quite so badly anymore, and,
overnight, nearly a quarter of them went out of business.

Ernie noted boarded-up gas stations on corner after corner,
and he wondered why the oil companies kept them boarded
up like that. Although they could use the underground tanks
for storage, the property wasn't producing any income on their
investment. Perhaps a gas company might be glad to get rid
of one of its surplus stations.

Ernie knew an opportunity when he saw it—he'd invested in homes and made money, and he'd purchased two apartment buildings in the past and done all right by himself—and he wasn't afraid to take a risk. He began to do some homework. Ernie called the real estate divisions of several major oil companies. Yes, they had a lot of stations and, yes, they would sell them or lease the land. They'd be thrilled if someone took one off their hands, and they weren't too particular about the price.

Next, Ernie began driving through many neighborhoods, looking for one that had a lot of condominiums or apartment buildings—in other words, a heavy concentration of people—but very few stores. He discovered that such areas weren't hard to find. Los Angeles was riddled with *major* shopping centers whose supermarkets had forced smaller markets out of business in the past. Now, many neighborhoods had no access to smaller grocery stores or, for that matter, to smaller drugstores and other types of stores, except at the major shopping centers.

The neighborhood Ernie found was perfect—no other small stores within a mile, no regional shopping center within four miles, and lots of apartments full of potential customers. The one type of outlet the neighborhood had in profusion was gas stations. Ernie found a nice closed station on a corner lot with access to busy streets. The station lot was about 25,000 square feet, slightly over half an acre.

Ernie approached the oil company and offered to buy the lot. The oil company representatives were shocked at first. They could see no useful purpose for the boarded-up station; but that was Ernie's problem, they reasoned, not theirs. After considerable haggling, they settled on a price of $1.50 per square foot, well below the average for commercial lots in the area. It would cost Ernie $37,500 to buy the lot, which he felt was a lot of money; so he began to back away.

When the oil company's property-management team saw they were losing a customer, they decided to sweeten the pot. They offered to sell the land to Ernie for only $10,000 down, and carry the balance themselves. (By leasing the land from them, he could have gotten it for virtually nothing down.)

Ernie said he wanted to put up several stores and asked if they would subordinate. Normally, they wouldn't, but they figured that the land was virtually useless to them, so they agreed.

Now, Ernie had his lot. His idea was to put up a small shopping center, or "strip" center, which meant that it would be a one-story building along the back portions of the lot. *Parking would be in front.* He anticipated getting four or five tenants, but first he had to have something to show—a picture of what he had in mind. (The saying that "a picture is worth a thousand words" is never more true than in investing. If you want people to know what you're talking about, don't tell them— show them.)

Architectural Costs—An "Up-front" Expense

Ernie had an architect draw up a tentative set of plans and a rendering of what the finished center would look like. The architect said that Ernie could pay him in one of three ways: he could pay a flat fee, a percentage of the eventual construction costs, or a certain amount per hour.

Ernie saw problems with all three billing methods. If he simply paid a flat fee, revisions could cost a great deal of money. On the other hand, if Ernie gave him a percentage of the construction costs, what incentive would there be for the architect to save money on building costs? And finally, if he paid by the hour, what assurance would he have that the architect wouldn't just loaf on the job?

Ernie's solution was a combination. He worked out an arrangement with the architect on a percentage of the total cost, not to exceed a set amount. It wasn't perfect, but Ernie felt assured he wouldn't be cheated.

The architect told Ernie that the city zoning and building departments would require sizable parking space for any structures he put up. He said that the usual formula was "4 to 1," which meant that for every square foot of building erected, Ernie would need four square feet of parking and driveways. Ernie did some quick arithmetic. On a 25,000-square-foot lot, his building could be only about 6,000 square feet.

"What if we go up?" Ernie asked. "If we build two stories, we can get 12,000 square feet."

"That's not really the case," the architect pointed out. "The city will require additional parking space for the second story. Also, my experience with other developers has been that two-story buildings are death. No one minds parking their car in front and walking right into a shop. But people won't stop if they have to walk up to a second floor. You'd never find tenants for the upstairs."

Ernie thought about arguing, but then decided that what had been said made sense. He asked the architect for a tentative set of plans.

"Fine," the architect agreed. "What kind of stores will you have—grocery, auto supply, drugs? Each has different requirements. And how big do you want them—all the same size, or some large and some small?"

Ernie felt himself getting angry. When he bought a house or an apartment building, there never had been any questions like this. For a moment he thought the architect might be trying to bait him, but then he realized the questions made perfect sense. Businesses had specific and different requirements. How could the architect be expected to come up with a set of plans until he knew what was going to go into the property?

But how could Ernie find any tenants without a set of plans to show? It seemed a no-win situation. Finally, Ernie said, "Just draw up a set of fantasy plans. Make one store about 2,500 square feet, like a small grocery, then make the rest smaller, about 800 or 900 square feet. That way, we'll end up with one large and four smaller stores."

The architect scowled. "I've been involved in speculative deals like this before. If you don't get tenants to fit, then you probably won't build, and I'll be out my time and effort, since we're on a percentage-of-cost basis. I'll draw up the plans on a per-hour basis now, to be paid upon completion. Then, if you decide to go ahead with the project later on, I'll deduct the amount you've paid me.

Ernie was forced to agree. It cost him an additional $1,000 out of pocket.

Finding Tenants

Ernie's next step was to fill his retail-store building with tenants. Once again, this was something totally new for him, and he soon found out he'd have to learn a great deal about retailing.

Ernie located a chain of small grocery stores and found out who represented them for acquisitions. He went to talk with her, Darlene. Darlene only gave him five minutes. Escorting him out the door, she offered Ernie some advice. "The next time you make a presentation," she said, "be sure you have all your information. You'll need a demographic breakdown of the number of potential customers in the drawing area, with their ages and income, and the rent you expect to get. You'll also need a sample lease, a plot plan of your lot, a traffic count of cars on the streets leading to your shopping center, and, if you expect to make a sale with us, an aerial map showing where your center is located and where all your competitors are! Finally, before taking up my time again, be sure you know exactly what our space and frontage requirements are, and be prepared to show us a drawing that fits our specific needs, not just a general architectural rendering!"

Ernie was speechless.

Figuring the Bottom Line

Discouraged, Ernie decided to figure out just what the profit of his shopping center would be, before he invested the money in the kind of presentation Darlene was talking about. He knew his land costs would be $1.50 per square foot, or $37,500. The architect had figured the cost of a building shell at about $25 per square foot, which meant an additional $150,000 into the property ($25/square foot × 6,000 sq. ft. = $150,000). He'd have about $190,000 into the shopping center by the time it was completed ($150,000 for building + $37,500 for lot = $187,500).

The question was: How much money could he make?

Ernie discovered that most strip centers in the area were leasing their space for between six and $12 per year per square foot. He decided to try to achieve a median figure of $9 per year. Since he had 6,000 square feet, Ernie could hope for $54,000 a year.

Ernie knew, of course, that there would be expenses for management, taxes, and insurance. (Although tenants pay their share of taxes and insurance with most modern leases, there is some common area of responsibility that falls to the owner.) Ernie guessed that his costs here would be about $4,000 per year, which left him a net annual income of $50,000. On the surface, a return of about 26% looked pretty good in terms of total investment.

Ernie, of course, had no intention of putting up all the money in cash. He had already borrowed $27,500 from the oil company, on an interest-only mortgage at 10%, which made his annual payments $2,750. He intended to borrow an additional $150,000 to put up the building. If the interest rate on that money were 14% for 30 years, his annual payments would be $21,000. The two mortgages had combined yearly payments of about $24,000.

		Payments	
First Mortgage of	$150,000	$21,300	per year
Second Mortgage	27,500	2,750	per year
	$177,500	$24,050	

If the $24,000 in mortgage debt were subtracted from his income, Ernie would be left with an actual yearly return (positive cash flow) of $26,000.

Net Income	$ 50,000
Mortgage Debt	24,000
Return	$ 26,000

Ernie had to look at the figures several times before he truly comprehended them. He was going to be making $26,000 a year. On the basis of his property costs ($187,500), that came to a return of about 14%; but on the basis of his actual investment ($10,000), that came to a return of 260%!

$$\frac{\$26,000 \quad \text{Actual Return}}{\$10,000 \quad \text{Total Investment}} = 260\%$$

Not only that, Ernie hadn't even figured what he could sell the property for. Using the net-income approach, he began scribbling figures to come up with a sales price. He knew that a return of 14% on net income (before calculating mortgage debt) was considered excellent at the time. He figured his property's value:

$$\frac{50,000 \quad \text{Net Income}}{.14} = \$357,143 \text{ value}$$

By this method of calculation, when the project was completed and rented, it would be worth over $350,000. That was nearly $170,000 more than the total cost—all of it pure profit! If a lower return (8%–12%) was used, an even higher value could be obtained.

Suddenly, Ernie felt his enthusiasm for the project returning. Getting the tenants and putting up the building would be a long haul, but now it all seemed worthwhile. The bottom-line potential was there.

With renewed energy, Ernie went back to his task. He found that it wasn't quite as hard to get aerial maps as he'd imagined. The government had photographed virtually every part of the country from one angle or another, and the maps were available from a variety of sources, including county road departments and federal agencies.

Finding the Demographics

Next, Ernie learned that information on the traffic count on the streets in front of his corner was available from local road and highway departments. He also checked with the U.S. Zip Code/Census Tract Direct Marketing Atlas (Data Publications, 24 E. Wesley Street, South Hackensack, New Jersey 07606), which analyzed markets by neighborhood clusters. Then he got copies of Current Population Reports (Bureau of the Census Library, Washington, D.C. 20233), which gave estimates of population, consumer income levels, education, and so forth. Finally, he checked with the local chamber of commerce for additional information.

When he was done, Ernie had an accurate profile of the area within a one-mile radius of his corner.

Population within One-Mile Radius of Proposed Strip Center
7,000 people

Age:	Under 6	6–13	14–17	18–24
	11%	10%	11%	9%
	25–34	35–49	50–64	65 & over
	23%	17%	12%	7%

By the time he had his demographics ready, Ernie also had a report on the street traffic. The count was high—over 4,500 cars during the 10 hours when businesses were most likely to remain open.

He also received his aerial maps and took a good look at the geography. He'd thought that a one-mile-population radius would look like a circle, with his store in the center; instead it appeared oblong, following the contours of the streets leading to his area. Ernie located his nearest competitors on the maps.

Then he received demographic information from the census department which gave him an income breakdown:

- Median income in his area—$17,000 per year
- Median family size—1.7

Ernie saw that his area was relatively affluent and that the family size was small, presumably because there were so many single people living in nearby apartments and condos. Ernie reasoned that singles would make more trips to a local grocery store (and eat out more) than large families, who would be more likely to go to a major shopping center for their food needs.

After confirming his decision to ask for $9 per square foot, per year, for his property, Ernie felt ready to tackle Darlene again.

Reluctantly, Darlene agreed to give him another fifteen minutes. This time it went much differently. Ernie showed Darlene the number of people, age composition, median income, and family makeup in the area of his proposed strip center. He pinpointed the car traffic and indicated the location of his nearest competitors on the aerial map. Additionally, he had the statistics to show that he was asking a fair rent.

Af the end of forty-five minutes, Darlene admitted that she was impressed. She said that her company would seriously consider renting space in the proposed building, depending, of course, on the lease terms that Ernie wanted. "By the way," she asked, "you're not going to insist on *ups* in the lease, are you? We won't accept ups."

Ernie had no idea what Darlene was talking about. Finally, he said, "It'll just be a standard lease."

"Standard?" Darlene looked at him suspiciously. "What's that?"

"Oh, you know," Ernie said, trying not to stumble, "the usual clauses."

"Let's get down to specifics," Darlene said. "You'll want a net, net, net lease, I presume, with a percentage of the gross, but no ups. Is that correct?"

Ernie nodded. He wasn't going to admit that he didn't know what she was talking about. But he decided that he would learn a lot more about leasing.

"Fine," Darlene said. "I think we can do business." She indicated that her company would lease 2,500 square feet of store space, and that she expected Ernie to build-to-suit. Her lease term would be for fifteen years, with options for four, five-year lease terms after that.

Terrific, thought Ernie, time to get started. His next step was the bank. He needed to borrow the money to get the building going and felt that he'd have an easy time of it. After all, he had a lease commitment for a major portion of his property. Ernie prepared a loan package as he'd been instructed by the loan officer of the bank he contacted (see Chapter 5).

The loan officer listened impatiently to Ernie's presentation. After about ten minutes, he interrupted Ernie and shook his head. "There's no way you can get financing on this."

Ernie was incredulous. "Why not?"

"Because it's a small strip center," the bank officer said. "Look, we're in the business of lending money; so we know something about risks. Small strip centers are a dime a dozen. You have to show us that your center is different—that your center will succeed where others have failed."

"How do I do that?" Ernie said, feeling defeated again.

"By giving us a strong anchor and strong subsidiary leases." Ernie shook his head. "An *anchor*," the bank officer explained, "is a strong lessee—like a bank, a savings and loan, a major drugstore chain or grocery-store chain. It anchors the shopping center and acts like a magnet to draw customers into the smaller stores. In your case, you have only a small grocery chain as your anchor. That's a start, but because it isn't a major store, we'll need to see all the other space leased before we'll consider a loan."

It was a setback, Ernie realized, but he wasn't exactly back to square one. He did have a firm lease commitment from his major tenant. Now all he had to do was to find minor tenants to fill the remaining stores.

Filling In the Tenancy Holes

That proved harder than it seemed at first. Because he had only small stores in a small strip center, Ernie could only appeal to small tenants. Likely prospects were a TV repair outlet, a liquor store, a camera shop, a key shop, a tobacconist, an ice cream parlor, and so on. But Ernie really had no idea which stores would be interested, and he wasn't sure how to find out.

His first tack was to consult publications that list tenants looking for shopping centers. Then he visited local stores to ask the owners if they were interested in expanding or moving. Finally, after securing a list from his local Realtor®'s Board, he consulted with real estate brokers who specialized in retail stores. In every case, Ernie was asked, "What kind of store will do well in your center?"

Ernie had to admit that he really wasn't sure, realizing that he had to know marketing (as well as the retailers) in order to learn which stores would prosper. For example, he had to know what kind of traffic a jewelry store would require, or a candy and nut store, or a liquor store. He had to understand the placement stores needed within the center, as well as the competition they wished to avoid.

Compounding his problems, Ernie had only a small area to work with. If he were dealing with a large shopping center, there would have been many potential tenants seeking to rent space, and he could have been choosy. With his small center, however, Ernie not only had to find a winning combination, he had to choose from what was available.

With great effort and perseverance, Ernie finally located four potential tenants: a coin laundry, a TV repair shop, a bike shop, and a small real estate office. He felt that his tenants would complement one another in several ways. During the day, traffic to the grocery store and laundry would probably be low, because most of their potential customers would be working. The bike shop, real estate office, and TV repair shop would bring in daytime business, and their clients would easily find room to park. On the other hand, these businesses would close at five, while the laundry and grocery outlet would remain open until midnight, with the parking area all to themselves during the evening. Additionally, Ernie felt the laundry and quick-service grocery store would complement each other, because people would drop in to buy a few items while their clothes were being washed. While the other stores didn't complement each other directly, they didn't seem to be in conflict. It seemed like a winning combination.

But when Ernie told them the rent, a couple balked. Ernie hadn't considered the different markups and volume of each business. If each business paid the same rent, some would be forced out of business, while others made huge profits. The real estate office could afford higher rent than the laundry, for example, simply because it did a higher volume in terms of gross sales. Similarly, the TV repair could pay higher rent than the bike shop. So Ernie ended up charging some tenants $12 per foot, and others only $6. His net rent remained approximately the same, and he helped assure the prosperity of his center by charging according to ability to pay.

One last problem loomed—all of Ernie's potential tenants were small-business people. While they indicated a willingness to move in once the center was built, completion was still six months away, and they were uncomfortable about making commitments so far into the future.

Ernie, however, couldn't get his loan without firm rental commitments, and ultimately, he had to play showdown with each tenant. After again pointing out the benefits of leasing in his center, Ernie insisted that the businesses sign a lease agreement and put up a small amount of "good faith" money to hold their place. All agreed except the real estate office, but Ernie was quickly able to find a substitute real estate company.

When Ernie went back to the bank, he brought concrete figures on rental income, signed lease agreements, and a firm estimate from a builder on construction costs. He thought he had it made.

The loan officer agreed that Ernie's package was complete and assured him that the bank would make the loan, subject to approval from its loan committee. He pointed out, however, that Ernie was applying for funds in a tight money market, and his bank (and others) was only making *exposed mortgages*.

Ernie had never heard the term and asked the officer to explain.

"Exposed mortgages is just a nickname. It means we'll only lend sixty-six percent of your land and construction costs on a construction loan, and then only if you have a commitment on a permanent loan."

Ernie did some quick calculations. He had $187,500 into the building and land; 66% of that was about $125,000. "That's not enough," he said. "It's $25,000 short of my construction costs."

The bank officer smiled. "That's why we call it an exposed loan. Part of your costs are exposed. You'll have to come up with the other $25,000 yourself."

Ernie was outraged. "I've met all your conditions," he said. "I've found tenants who've signed agreements. There's a lot of money to be made in this project, and you're telling me you still won't go ahead with full financing?"

This time the officer scowled. "It's simply a matter of risk.

There's more risk in small strip centers, regardless of how well they look. If times were better we'd loan up to 80%; but today, 66% is the best we can do. If you don't like it, I suggest you check with other lenders, but I think you'll find the story pretty much the same."

Ernie took the loan. He also made a great deal of money. He had plenty of problems along the way. The contractor he hired to build the shopping center, for example, turned out to be more of a credit risk than Ernie was. He filed for bankruptcy, which tied up the building for another three months while Ernie moved to free his property from liens the builder's creditors had attached to it.

And just before he was ready to open, the grocery-store chain backed out of its commitment, forfeiting its earnest money, but leaving Ernie high and dry without a major tenant. Fortunately, a small pharmacy chain was looking for a site in just such a location, and Ernie was able to re-lease his building.

Ernie discovered both the headaches and the money to be found in shopping center investments. After two years he raised rents, and eventually he sold the center for over half a million dollars. Ernie's profit was more than a quarter-million dollars on an investment that, ultimately, was less than $40,000 in cash.

WHAT IT TAKES TO SUCCEED

Can anyone do what Ernie did?

Recently, small strip centers were hot; tomorrow, something else will be booming. There's always opportunity, but a lot depends on finding a good location, getting tenants and financing, and hooking up with a good architect and a solid builder. Most of all, success depends on your own temperament. In shopping centers, as nowhere else in real estate, those who are successful might best be described as dreamers. When everyone is ready to throw in the towel—because the city won't allow a variance in an ordinance, a lender won't make a loan, or the rain has washed out the building site—the shopping center developer says, "It will pass, and when it does, I'll get it done and make a bundle."

Understanding Retailers

Ernie obtained a modicum of understanding of the retailing business by spending a few concentrated months in learning its problems. An expert developer, however, needs years of experience in various retail fields before he fully understands how to match a retailer with the right shopping center.

In larger regional centers, for example, there is almost a science devoted to *location*—the placement of the appropriate retailer in the right spot in the center. It involves knowing, for example, that jewelers can afford high rent on their Gross Leasable Area (GLA) but rarely need much space. Consequently, they tend to get stuck out in front, or in nooks and crannies too small for other retailers. Additionally, some stores complement each other, while others detract from one another. I've seen good managers improve the income of faltering shopping centers by 40%, simply by rearranging store locations.

Another area of understanding has to do with combining demographics with the *type* of store. In today's two-income families, for example, many more people eat out than before, greatly enlarging the opportunities for a variety of restaurants. Some regional shopping centers even have a restaurant row in which all the food businesses are located.

As we move away from the small strip center and into larger buildings, *design* becomes increasingly critical. Large buildings require pillars or posts for support, and while many retailers will accept a pillar or post near the back of the store, nobody will tolerate one near the front. A pillar breaks up counter space, distracts customers and, worst of all, cuts down on visibility.

Visibility is a key word to retailers, which usually means lots of glass and the opportunity to put up a big sign. In strip centers, where each store faces the street, it means a sign at least two feet high. Inside a shopping center, it means a sign that can quickly distinguish the retailer from other sellers. The

smart developer, or shopping center purchaser, will consult
the retailer as well as the architect in designing the building.
In most cases, the retailer knows what visibility he or she
requires in order to sell.

The list of retailer requirements is a lengthy one, and those
who want more information on the subject should check the
source material at the end of the chapter.

Understanding Retailer Economics

Shopping center developers or investors should understand
how and when retailers *expand*. After all, though some tenants
move into a shopping center simply to improve their location,
many others are retailers expanding their businesses by opening
a new outlet.

While each type of business is different, it's probably fair to
say that retailers are involved in inventory the way developers
are involved in property. Inventory is the retailer's stock in
trade. Sales staff and management are very important, but
without inventory the retailer has nothing to sell and is out of
business. Therefore, in order to expand, a retailer must be able
to completely stock a new store, and that costs a great deal of
money. The key to finding that money for the retailer may also
be the key to finding a successful tenant for the shopping
center developer.

Borrowing is usually the cleanest method for the retailer to
find additional funds. If the bank will lend enough money to
buy the inventory, the retailer will be in a position to open a
new outlet. That's easier said than done, however. Retailers
operate on strict margins (markups). In order to justify their
rent, they must produce a certain income for each square foot
of space. They also have to remain competitive to stay in business. If they have to borrow to buy their inventory, the interest
on the loan must be added to their margin; so they must charge
more or pay less rent in order to break even. Either way, *borrowing* to expand is difficult for the retailer.

"Floating" Inventory

Consequently, retailers have developed a method of expanding that uses "free" money—money on which they pay no interest. It's called a *float*, and it operates like a traveler's check. When we pay a quarter on the traveler's check we buy, many of us think that the quarter is the bank's profit. Nothing could be farther from the truth. The quarter simply helps defray the cost of writing out the check.

The profit comes from the float. When we buy a traveler's check, the check's sponsor receives instant cash. But we may not spend the check until weeks later. The float is the period between the time we buy and spend the traveler's check. During that time, the check's sponsor has free use of our money—they lend it out or invest it, and therein lies the profit.

When we consider the hundreds of thousands of people who buy traveler's checks each year, we can understand how the income of traveler's check companies rivals that of the world's largest banks. It is perhaps the single most lucrative business in the world—and it all depends on the float!

Retailers can sometimes use the float in a similar fashion. It all has to do with how fast a retailer can turn over merchandise. An aggressive record dealer, for example, can turn over his inventory in as little as 30 to 45 days. Yet, during easy money periods, that same retailer may have 90 days in which to pay a wholesaler for his merchandise. That leaves him with 45 days to float the interest-free cash however he chooses. And many retailers use the float time to buy additional merchandise and open new outlets.

When interest rates are low, wholesalers try to entice retailers into ordering more goods by increasing the time for repayment, often to 90 days or even longer. During such loose money periods, retailers may be eager to expand. When money is tight and interest rates high, however, these same wholesalers, who have to borrow money to build their products, now want payment as soon as possible, often within 10 to 30 days.

Understanding retailers, and their ability or nonability to float inventory, is critical to the success or failure of many shopping centers. Trying to develop a center during tight money times may be virtually impossible, simply because retailers won't be able to expand. It's all part of the shopping center game.

Financing

Financing is another vital part of the game. Whether it's a tiny shopping center such as Ernie built, or a super-regional center, the only real difference in terms of financing is the amount of money and who's offering it.

As of this writing, lenders are reviewing their requirements for shopping center loans and adding a few new items. Most want "ups"—a lease clause in which the amount paid increases according to the inflation rate, as measured by the Consumer Price Index (CPI). The lenders want to make a secure profit, which means they want a rate of return two to four percent above the rate of inflation. If inflation this year is ten percent, for example, they'll want a rate of return of 12 to 14 percent, or they won't make the loan.

Increased costs of financing ultimately result in higher rents, reducing the number of potential tenants. Consequently, we'll probably see far fewer shopping centers built in the future than we have in the past. (There are probably over 20,000 medium- to large-sized shopping centers in the United States, and at least as many strip centers.)

To get around today's problems of financing, we're seeing two different kinds of solutions. The first is *creative financing*, which means that the seller of the land helps finance the shopping center, in order for it to succeed. The second solution is the *convertible* loan. This is a loan which initially bears a relatively low interest rate, and is, therefore, particularly appealing to the shopping center developer. It includes an option, however, by which the lender can become the owner. Thus, if the shopping center doesn't do well, the lender simply collects interest. But if the center does particularly well, the lender can buy the center for an agreed-upon fee. Convertible loans appeal to pension-fund lenders, who can buy and then sell, and take a capital-gains tax advantage.

SHOPPING CENTER TYPES

I've saved this discussion for last, because I think it's more meaningful once we know what we're talking about. Our example with Ernie introduced us to shopping centers in general. Now let's break them down into specifics.

Most people involved in shopping centers break them into five distinct categories, in terms of their minimum-support population, size of building and land, and the type of store contained within.

Center Type	Store Type (Anchor)	Land Area	Support Pop.
Strip center	small independent	½–1 acre	5,000
Neighborhood	small chain	3 acres	30,000
City	large chain grocery or drug	10–12 acres	75–100,000
Regional	one–two large department stores	35 acres	250,000
Super-regional	three or more department stores	over 50 acres	over 350,000

Naturally, there are far more of the smaller types of shopping centers than the larger ones. However, there are well over 1,000 regional centers in the United States. We've discussed some of the opportunities with the smaller centers; now let's consider the opportunities with the larger centers.

In general, unless you are well established in the shopping center field, with at least a five- to ten-year track record, you won't be able to muster the support (financial, leasing, retailer, etc.) to put up a regional shopping center. There are, however, many individuals with sizable sums to invest who would be interested in a regional center. Surely there must be some way for them to become involved. There is.

First, let's look at the profit potential. In today's market, a regional shopping center developer can expect to pay between $4–$6 a square foot, just for the land (and remember, perhaps three-fourths of the land will end up in parking area). In addition, building costs will be far higher for a regional center than for a smaller one. In a regional center there are often two or three floors, with elevators and covered interiors adding to the expense. Presently, *building costs* run about $40 per square foot for the GLA with the non-revenue-producing area—perhaps 40% of total interior area—costing closer to $65 per square foot. And costs are rising.

Of course, rents in a regional center also tend to be higher. In addition to taxes, insurance and maintenance, tenants pay the developer close to $20 per square foot, plus $5 per square foot to cover the non-revenue-producing areas. Developers generally aim for a spendable profit, after all expenses are paid, of about $3 per square foot. Since some regional centers cover well over a million square feet, it's easy to see that there are big bucks to be made here.

(*Note:* Earlier we saw that second stories don't work well in small shopping centers. What doesn't work small, however, may work big. Many regional centers are built on rolling land with entrances on different levels, which helps offset the idea of upper and lower floors. Nevertheless, even in regional centers, retailers on the lower floor tend to do more business than those on upper floors.)

The easiest way for an inexperienced investor to get into a regional shopping center is to form a partnership with a developer. Developers are always looking for partners with capital, and with limited liability available through syndication, this becomes a highly appealing opportunity.

SHOPPING CENTER OPPORTUNITIES IN THE MID-1980S

Presently, there continue to be strong opportunities for profits with small, "strip" shopping centers and with the larger regional centers. Of course, new centers and increased value for older ones will depend, in large part, on the availability of mortgage money and the overall state of the American economy.

Of particular interest to investors with sizable capital is a new concept in shopping centers—the *inner city* shopping center. This is a center which occupies the bottom two or three floors of a large (or even high-rise) building, while the upper floors are devoted to office space.

These centers are prospering as a direct result of the energy crisis facing all industrial countries. While suburban centers must rely almost exclusively on auto traffic for their support, inner city centers rely on foot, bus, and train (subway) service, in addition to automobile traffic. Further, with their high density of population, the inner cities give these centers the largest possible number of people on which to draw.

These inner city centers are extraordinarily costly, with land prices of several hundred dollars per square foot, and with exorbitant building costs because of the vertical nature of the structure. The returns, however, are also very high. Because of the mix of office and shopping center space, and because of the enormous area covered by the many floors in the building, inner city centers can return as much as $4 to $5 per square foot!

The following publications are helpful in providing names of developers, brokers and investors, as well as giving locations of shopping centers which are for sale.

Shopping Center World Magazine
6285 Barfield Road
Atlanta, Georgia 30328
This is the granddaddy of publications in this field. It is a big, thick magazine, often over 300 pages in length, that has just about everything in it.

Western Real Estate News
3057 17th Street
San Francisco, California 94110
This is a smaller publication that caters primarily to the West Coast. It has helpful information on specific projects.

Chain Store Age Magazine
425 Park Avenue
New York, New York 10022
Gives information on many retailers, which can be helpful when you're looking for tenants.

Southwest Real Estate News
11325 Pegasus, Suite W-158
Dallas, Texas 75238

This is a monthly tabloid with news of recent real estate and shopping center developments.

Shopping Center Directory
424 North Third
Burlington, Iowa 52601

This is basically a listing of nearly all the shopping centers in the United States.

Retailer's Guide to Shopping Center Leasing
National Retail Merchants Association
100 West 31st Street
New York, New York 10001

This small book is very helpful when learning how to negotiate a lease. It also gives information on design, terms and risk from the tenants' point of view.

Directory of Regional Malls
Shopping Center Digest
Box 2
Suffern, New York 10901

This lists Canadian and U.S. malls.

Franchise Opportunities Handbook
U.S. Commerce Department
Superintendent of Documents
U.S. Government Printing Office
Washington, D.C. 20402

This lists over a thousand retailers who specifically franchise outlets.

Chapter Ten

LEASING INVESTMENT PROPERTY

Knowing something about leases can make a big difference in our ability to succeed in investment real estate. If you buy a house to rent out, the lease may be the least of your headaches. Many owners simply buy a form lease from the neighborhood stationery store and fill in the blanks. (That is not recommended—a lease prepared by an attorney for your unique situation is always best.) But if you buy or build a shopping center, it should be apparent that a lease is far more critical. The lease, in fact, can be a determining factor in whether or not you show a profit. Much the same holds true when leasing office or professional space, as we'll see in the next chapter.

LEASE TYPES

Leases, generally, are one of two types, the first of which is the *ground* lease—as the name implies, what's being rented is the ground. It's frequently used when the lease term is long, say, 50 or 99 years. The landowner leases the property to a developer, who then puts up a shopping center, office building, or whatever, and who pays rent on the leased property. For the landowner, the nice thing about a ground lease is that, when the lease term expires, all the buildings revert in ownership to the property. With a store or *building* lease, on the other hand, a tenant (such as a store owner) rents space from a building owner. It's the type of lease Ernie offered in the last chapter; it's also the type we'll be discussing here.

(*Note:* Both types of leases can be combined, or "sandwiched." For example, a developer can lease land, then put up a building and give leases to tenants.)

Primitive Leases

A basic lease involves two parties—the tenant, or lessee, and the landlord, or lessor. It stipulates that a certain sum of money is to be paid in regular installments to the landlord, for which the tenant is allowed to occupy space. That's basically the agreement. It's the fine print which determines whether the landlord or the tenant is going to make any money on the lease.

Forty years ago, or earlier, the fine print was not a consideration in commercial leases. By that I mean that the rental amount to be paid each month was fixed. If the lessee agreed to pay fifty cents per square foot for 2,000 square feet, the landlord could expect $1,000 in rent each month—as long as the lessee didn't go broke, he could bank on it. This agreement was called a *gross* lease.

But landlords soon realized that they were losing money with this kind of lease. The tenant simply paid a fixed amount of money. But the landlord had to pay taxes on the property, insurance on the building, and the costs of maintenance. And, adding insult to injury, the costs of taxes, insurance and maintenance were always rising.

The landlord with a lease for fifty cents per square foot soon learned it was costing him ten cents per square foot in these expenses; so his net rental income was really only forty cents per square foot. And because these costs were going up, he could see that next year his net income might be down to thirty-eight cents a square foot, or lower. It was a losing proposition for him each month.

It was also a loser in terms of value. (You'll recall that the value of commercial investment property is determined on the basis of *net* income, and the way to increase value is to increase net income.) With these primitive leases, the net income went down each year instead of up, and the property became less valuable.

At the end of the lease period, of course, the landlord could insist on higher rents, but that was inefficient, since most good tenants preferred long-term leases. Many wanted leases of 15 or 20 years, so they could be locked into a location. They didn't want to spend a great deal of money promoting a store, only to lose the location because their lease had expired and the landlord decided to rent to someone else.

The Net Lease

To solve the problem of diminishing net income landlords created the *net* lease, which transferred the rising costs of taxes, insurance, and maintenance to the tenant. If, for example, a landlord charged fifty cents per square foot in rent and paid ten cents per square foot in expenses, his net rental income was forty cents per square foot under the terms of an old lease. With a *net* lease, the landlord would charge forty cents per square foot, but the tenant would now be responsible for the costs of taxes, insurance and maintenance.

Say the tenant occupies 2,000 square feet of a 10,000-square-foot building. The yearly expenses for the building look like this:

Taxes	$ 5,000
Insurance	1,000
Maintenance	4,000
Total expenses	$10,000

The total annual expenses on the building for taxes, insurance and maintenance are $10,000. Since our tenant occupies 20 percent of the building, he is responsible for 20 percent of these expenses, or $2,000:

$10,000   Total expenses
×   20%   Space occupied
$ 2,000   Tenant liability

Under the terms of a net lease, at the end of the year the tenant must pay this $2,000, *in addition* to the base rental fee. The advantage to the landlord is obvious—a net rental income which does not decrease as expenses go up. As the costs of taxes, insurance and maintenance rise, these increases are borne by the tenant. This also helps the landlord calculate and enhance the market value of his building.

The net lease is pretty much standard across the country today. It is often called the "net, net, net" lease, or "3 net," which means that all three items—taxes, insurance and maintenance—are covered.

The Percentage Lease

At first, landlords were satisfied with the net lease. Their income was no longer decreasing as costs went up. Until it came time to renegotiate the lease, however, their properties were not increasing in value. This, they reasoned, was not fair.

For example, let's say we have a shopping center in which there are ten stores doing a combined business (gross sales volume) of one million dollars a year. And let's say that their gross income doubles in three years. Presumably, the shopping center has become more desirable to customers, and is, therefore, more valuable. But because rental rates do not reflect this increase in business, the price at which a developer/owner could sell this center does not increase.

Landlords again found a creative solution to their dilemma. They came up with the *percentage* lease. In this lease, the tenant agrees to pay rent based, in part, on the gross sales of the store. It can be handled in one of three ways: (1) in most shopping centers, figures are specified for a minimum rental rate and for a percentage of gross sales, and the tenant pays the greater of the two; or (2) the tenant may simply pay a percentage of gross sales; or finally, the tenant may pay a fixed minimum rent, plus a specific percentage of gross sales above an agreed-upon figure.

This second-generation lease was what everyone wanted in the 1950s and 1960s. If you owned a shopping center that didn't have percentage leases and you wanted to sell, no one would buy. "Does the property have percentage leases?" was the first question asked. Landlords with percentage leases thought they were sitting pretty and had nothing to worry about. Then came the inflation of the late seventies and early eighties, and new problems hit commercial property. Many of the problems caused by inflation are related to the cost of borrowing money. Inflation doesn't mean that products and labor get more valuable; it means that money gets less valuable.

In terms of shopping centers and other commercial properties in the 1980s, this means that developers and investors must be able to pay flexible interest rates. The days when a lender would accept 8% interest for 30 years are long gone. Today's lenders want short-term mortgages at flexible interest rates. If inflation soars, lenders want to be able to get more interest.

Landlords with percentage leases are suddenly getting alarmed. True, they get more money as sales go up, but now that money is less valuable. Additionally, they may be faced with increased mortgage payments.

Indexed Leases

Landlords have responded to this latest crisis by creating the *indexed* lease. In addition to a net and a percentage, today's landlords want the amount of money paid by the tenants to be keyed to an indicator of money's value, generally the Consumer Price Index (CPI). Most tenants, however, say they would rather not rent than accept an indexed lease. Their fear is understandable—with such a lease, they would have no control over how much rent they may ultimately be committed to.

The solution to the landlord/tenant confrontation over indexing may be found in the use of an index other than the CPI (which is notoriously weighted in favor of the consumer). Many are suggesting that rentals be keyed to the Wholesale Price Index, or even to the cost of funds as indicated by the Federal Home Loan Bank Board, or the Federal Reserve.

Indexing is the key to the lease of the future and should not be overlooked by anyone considering leasing today. There may come a time when it will simply be impossible to sell a shopping center, or other commercial property, unless it has an indexed lease. (In the vernacular, an indexed lease is called *ups*, which means that the rent goes up and up and up.)

TYPICAL CLAUSES IN COMMERCIAL LEASES

Although we've just traced a short history of the commercial lease, we've really only skimmed the surface of leasing. Commercial leases may be more than a hundred pages in length and contain thousands of clauses, each related to a specific area of performance and payment. Here are some typical clauses found in commercial leases.

Alterations

This is a clause which usually specifies what types of alterations to the premises may be done by the tenant. It is important to the lessor, because it prevents the tenant from widely changing the design or structure of the property, thereby making it unleasable in the future.

Competition

This is a clause in commercial and shopping center leases which can work in one of two ways. In the first, the tenant may agree not to operate another, similar business within a specific distance (a three-mile radius, for example) from the location leased. The second use of this clause protects the tenant from the landlord. The owner of an Italian restaurant, for example, may insist that the landlord sign a competition clause, specifying that no other Italian restaurants will be allowed in the same shopping center. In actual practice, however, few landlords will sign such competition clauses, which is why we see half a dozen shoe outlets or jewelry stores in large shopping centers—all in direct competition with one another.

Common Area Contributions

This clause is increasingly found in shopping center leases, particularly for large centers with malls. Since the common area—the enclosed walkways or mall area—often amounts to forty percent of the overall floor space, maintaining these areas can be very expensive. In a common-area-contribution clause, the tenants agree to reimburse the owner for their share of such expenses, based on the ratio of the area they lease to the total shopping center area. In large shopping centers, this can amount to $5 or more per square foot leased and is a serious consideration for prospective tenants.

Construction

This clause covers new construction within a shopping center to be done either by or for a new tenant, specifying what is to be built and how it is to be paid for. Since the landlord retains possession of the premises after the lease term expires and the tenant moves, the landlord usually pays for building costs. So this clause normally would spell out whether the tenant would handle the construction and be reimbursed by the landlord, or whether the landlord would build, and the maximum costs he would assume.

Sales Percentage

This paragraph specifies on what basis the percentage of the lease will be determined—gross sales, net, or other. Usually, it also provides the landlord with the right to inspect the tenant's books—to corroborate the accuracy of the figures.

Parking Areas

This clause specifies any additional amounts the tenant must pay for maintenance of the parking areas, as well as any parking restrictions.

Relocation Right by Landlord

This is a clause on which landlords usually insist, and against which tenants usually fight. It gives the landlord, upon proper notice, the right to move the tenant to a different area of the building. Landlords want the freedom to place their tenants in what they consider complementary locations. Tenants, however, frequently distrust the developer's judgment and don't want to move from what they consider a terrific spot. As a compromise, such clauses sometimes give the tenant the right to refuse to move, unless a penalty (perhaps of a certain sum of money) is paid by the landlord.

Security Deposit

This is a standard clause in almost all leases, whether commercial or residential. It is simply a certain sum of money which the tenant puts up to cover repair and breakage to the property. If the tenant leaves the property in good condition, excepting normal wear and tear, all or part of this amount is usually returned.

Sign Installation

This specifies the type, size, brightness, location, and maintenance of the sign the tenant may install. Since it is one of the retailer's biggest drawing cards (hooks), the sign is of great importance to both tenant and landlord.

Other Clauses

There are, of course, a great many other clauses that go into leases. There are such legal clauses as warranties by landlord and tenant, legal description of property, penalties for default, and so on. Other clauses detail the landlord's right to enter the premises, the tenant's need to join a shopping center merchants' association (which helps oversee operation of the property), remodeling and repair clauses, and so on.

We've covered here some of the clauses that reveal how a lease operates. For advice on the inclusion and wording of clauses in any lease you may be contemplating—whether landlord or tenant—you should consult with an attorney. The lease is the vehicle which carries virtually every type of commercial real estate. In the next chapter, we'll see how leases function in professional and office buildings.

Chapter Eleven

INVESTING IN AN OFFICE BUILDING

An office building can be one of the most profitable of real estate investments. Opportunities in this market have been swelling in the United States since the early 1970s; and with the high interest rates that caused a construction slowdown in the early 1980s, demand for office-building space appears to be fast outdistancing supply. Until we see another big surge in construction, the market for this investment is likely to remain strong.

ADVANTAGES TO THE INVESTOR

The advantages of office buildings over other types of real estate can be broken down into four areas:

1) When we buy an office building, we have one enormous advantage over investors in residential property—all of our tenants (presumably) are business people. As such, they are familiar with contracts and leases, and usually have a good idea of their incomes and expenses. More importantly, should they be unable to make their payments because of business setbacks, we don't mind evicting them as much as we might a family whose breadwinner had just lost a job and couldn't

153

make the payments on a house we own. Perhaps the biggest single advantage of office buildings over residential real estate is that they are "cleaner"—there's less danger of getting emotionally involved with the tenants.

2) Office buildings are usually large enough for the owner to hire a manager, which further limits the owner's involvement and makes for a professionally run, real estate project.

3) Lenders are even more familiar with office buildings than they are with shopping centers. Success for office buildings, overall, is much higher than for shopping centers, so lenders are usually more willing to make loans on them.

4) With the right market and location, profit opportunities in office buildings are as high, or higher, than for almost any other type of real estate.

FINDING THE PROFIT

Since profit is normally the motive underlying any commercial real estate investment, let's see where profit is to be made in office buildings. One person who found out was Arlene.

Arlene had made some money in residential real estate and now wanted to move up to bigger investments. She decided to invest in an office building, but had little idea of how or where to make her investment. So she followed what many have used to ride their way to fortune—her good common sense.

Arlene assumed the role of a business-woman looking to rent 500 square feet of office space. She looked in the local paper, checked with brokers specializing in office buildings, and drove down to the business district of the city, looking for signs that said Office to Let.

Location!

In the course of a few weeks, Arlene made some important discoveries. She found that everyone talked *location* when it came to office space. For tenants, the right location seemed critical. Owners and brokers took great pains to emphasize that a particular area was in a good location.

But just what was a good location? She wanted to know.

Everyone seemed to divide office space into two general areas. One was the Central Business District (CBD). In this large city, there was a main CBD and another, slightly smaller, yet newer CBD at the outskirts of town. The second general area was all the space for rent "outside" the CBD (OCBD), including office space in the suburbs as well as on streets leading into the CBD.

The strange thing, Arlene quickly discovered, was that while everyone agreed on two distinct areas of office space, they didn't agree on which was better. Some businesses preferred the CBD, others the OCBD; some desired high-rise towers, while others wanted small, "friendly" buildings; some wanted locations on well-traveled streets, while others preferred side streets.

This phenomenon of diverse preference was reflected, Arlene noted, in both the cost of rental space and the vacancy rate. It cost about the same (within 20%) to rent in the CBD as in the OCBD. There were exceptions, of course, with newer, more desirable buildings charging much higher than average rents, and with older, less desirable ones charging much lower rents. Overall, however, the rents were surprisingly similar, regardless of location.

Vacancy rates, too, seemed unrelated to location. Because high interest rates had curtailed construction in the city, there was a strong demand but little excess supply. Brokers estimated that the overall vacancy rate, regardless of whether it was the CBD or the OCBD, was down below two percent, which was reflected by the recent rise in office rents. A year earlier, the average rent was ninety-five cents per square foot per month; since then the average had risen to $1.05 per square foot, and everyone talked about further increases.

From her observations, Arlene formulated a rule for investing in office buildings during the 1980s: *Location is important with every type of real estate; but with office buildings, it's not as important as the levels of supply and demand.* Because of the shortage of office space in her city, coupled with the strong demand for it from business people and professionals, Arlene was convinced that there was an opportunity for her in this market.

From her earlier investments, Arlene had about $200,000 to invest in an office building. First she considered the CBD in the main downtown area, composed largely of older, three- to seven-story buildings. When she inquired, she found that their prices were in the tens of millions of dollars, and because they were old, most needed some major repair or refurbishing. Although such an investment appeared too rich for her blood, Arlene continued to investigate and learned that the profit opportunities in the main CBD were indeed enormous.

People were returning to the central city (at least where the crime rates weren't the highest), and they were looking for good, renovated office-building space. The investor with the capital to purchase one of these run-down buildings at a bargain price, then totally refurbish it into modern office space, often found that he or she could quickly resell at an enormous profit. Arlene discovered investors who were doing just that.

Matching the Property to the Pocketbook

Arlene's problem, however, was money—unless she found a particularly small building (possible if she looked long enough), she'd need a million dollars or more to get involved in such a project. In addition, she would have to sustain the mortgage payments, taxes, insurance and other costs during refurbishing, when there would probably be no income.

Arlene decided to look at the newer CBD, which had been built near the edge of the city. But there she found mostly large, high-rise office buildings, which had been built at enormous expense and commanded the highest rents in the city. Most of the investors there, Arlene discovered, were large financial organizations, insurance companies, pension funds, and a very few wealthy individuals. She quickly declined the new CBD.

That left only the OCBD, which Arlene investigated next. In the Green Valley area, she found a strong need for office space. This new community at the outskirts of the city was still relying for much of its services on the city itself. A large number of new homes had been built over the past several years, and there was a new shopping center. For office space, however, most business people had to look elsewhere. To Arlene it seemed an opportunity, but she found the few available buildings to be too highly priced.

The First Alternative—Building

Arlene then checked for lots zoned for office-building space. Though many were available, the owners wanted fairly substantial prices for them. Arlene decided to calculate the profit potential on a lot she found on Marble Street, which was priced at $450,000. She consulted an architect, who said that it could cost about $40 a square foot to build, and that the city would allow a maximum, 10,000-square-foot building on the lot, which came to another $400,000. Building and lot together would cost $850,000.

If she could rent the building out for $1 per foot per month, assuming no vacancies, her monthly income would be $10,000, $120,000 annually. Subtracting $20,000 for expenses still left her with $100,000, or a 12% return (roughly) on total cost.

$$\frac{100,000}{850,000} = 12\%$$

Then Arlene considered the financing. With $200,000 in cash, she would need financing for $650,000. On a mortgage of $650,000 at 14% interest, her loan payment would be $92,352. That only left her an actual income (positive cash flow) on the building of $7,648, or about 4% on her investment of $200,000.

$100,000 net income − $92,352 mortgage payment = $7,648

$$\frac{\$7,648 \text{ cash back}}{\$200,000 \text{ investment}} = 3.8\%$$

From a builder she consulted, Arlene learned that there would be "soft" costs in addition to the hard costs of building materials, land and labor. During construction, she would have to pay interest on the construction loan, plus taxes and insurance on the property. Further, she probably would have to fight city hall to get her building plans approved, and perhaps hire a lawyer and even a public-relations firm. It all could add another $100,000 to her expenses.

Arlene threw up her hands, feeling that it just wasn't worth it. (She didn't know that many highly experienced architects, brokers and contractors will form partnerships with a prospective investor on just such a project, particularly if the investor has first located and tied up a good piece of property.)

Another Alternative—Conversion

When she had just about reached her wits' end, however, It was a run-down, two-story building on what had once been a major artery through Green Valley. A recently built expressway had cut off the two-lane road, which now served as the major street for the business district of the area. The business district was small—just a few stores and shops about ten blocks away from the motel. Arlene stumbled on the place only because she first thought it was an office building, with a For Sale by Owner sign on it. She realized it was a motel only after she turned around and drove in.

The motel owner, who had bought the place during its heyday, when the road in front was also a major thoroughfare for visitors, was barely hanging on and ready to sell. The owner was apologetic about the condition of his property, pointing out that a little money and some elbow grease could turn it once again into a first-rate motel. He didn't mention that the lack of through-traffic on the street made it an exceptionally poor location for a motel.

There were twenty units, ten on each floor, with an outside walkway on one side of the building leading to each. The walkway faced a parking area, and there was additional parking in back.

The owner showed Arlene his profit-loss statement for the last year, and she noted that his net income was only $20,000. He shrugged and said, "That's the motel business." When she asked, the motel owner said he wanted $250,000 for his property.

Arlene thanked him and then checked with a local broker, who thought the motel was probably worth $195,000 if someone could operate it at all. There just wasn't much need for the motel, now that it was bypassed by the freeway. Most of the travelers to the area stayed at the newer, larger motels, near the expressway off-ramps. Arlene next checked with the city zoning commission. The motel was currently zoned for hotel/ motel use, but the city had been accepting zoning changes to commercial/office use of late, because of demand in the area for office space. The representative she talked with said that there was an excellent chance of rezoning.

Arlene decided to take a chance. She offered the owner of the Moonlight Motel full price, if he would accept an offer contingent upon her getting the zoning change. The owner was skeptical that the city would make a change. He'd been around long enough to know that zoning-commission policies were strict. "They won't give a little person a chance," he said.

"Have you gone down and tried?" Arlene asked.

The owner had to admit he hadn't, but he was certain they wouldn't change the zoning. And he wouldn't sign a contingency offer.

Arlene took back her offer and thought about it. The people at the zoning commission had been optimistic about her chances of rezoning the Moonlight Motel. If it were rezoned, then she could convert it from a motel to an office building. The change of use should allow her to make a profit—she decided to find out just how much.

Each motel room was about 300 square feet, including a bathroom (fortunately, there were no kitchen units). Three hundred square feet times 20 units gave her a total of 6,000 square feet. If she could rent it out for slightly below the going rate, say, ninety cents per square foot, she should be able to bring in about $5,400 a month. Assuming she leased out the units on net leases and allowed $500 a month for other expenses, her net income should be about $4,900 a month, or $58,800 a year.

Arlene quickly calculated that this net income (assuming a cap rate of 12%) made the property worth about half a million dollars.

$$\frac{58,800}{.12} = \$490,000$$

If she could get it for anywhere near the asking price and make the conversion, she could do very well indeed. Arlene decided to take a gamble. She said that she would buy the motel, if the owner would reduce his price to $200,000. But, the owner was adamant. He said he needed $250,000 for his retirement. Exasperated, Arlene made a final offer, $225,000, and the owner grabbed it.

Getting the Property—The First Battle of the War

By putting up $100,000 in cash and having the owner carry back a note for the balance, Arlene had her motel. But that was just the beginning. Now she had to petition the zoning commission and provide an environmental impact report on the zoning change. She had to get approval from surrounding businesses (which were happy to see the motel go), and finally, she had to get zoning approval. The entire process took eight months, during which she ran up an additional $12,000 interest on the mortgage to the former owner of the Moonlight Motel, plus another $6,000 in taxes and other expenses. But at last she got her approval.

During the next three months, Arlene refurbished the motel. She put an ornate railing on the walkways in front of the rooms and hung potted plants around it. She recarpeted and paneled the rooms, had the air conditioning repaired, and replaced some of the parking in front with a garden. (Fortunately, she had extra parking available in back, because the city required one parking space per office unit.)

It was nearly a year before Arlene was ready to rent the new Green Valley Garden offices for $1.00 a foot (by then, nearby office space was renting for $1.15 a foot; so she figured she could afford to charge more). Because she was located where there was little other available office space, the offices filled up almost immediately.

Arlene found that leases for office use were somewhat different from those for shopping centers or residential property, with which she was familiar. She asked for and got a net lease, but she had to provide all the maintenance and upkeep for the common areas, and she didn't receive a percentage of business.

She did manage, however, to get a clause inserted in all leases running three years or longer, which allowed her to renegotiate the lease amount each year, based on the CPI.

Arlene was soon collecting a net of about $5,400 a month, or $64,800 annually—assuming a 12% cap rate, that made her property worth $540,000.

$$\frac{64,800}{.12} = \$540,000$$

She then calculated her costs. Her soft costs—her mortgage payments during the fight with the city and the remodeling period—came to roughly $20,000. Refurbishing costs added another $120,000.

COSTS OF CONVERTING THE MOONLIGHT MOTEL INTO THE GREEN VALLEY GARDEN OFFICES

Soft costs (interest, taxes, insurance, etc.)	$ 20,000
Hard costs (remodeling)	120,000
Purchase price	225,000
Total Costs	365,000
Estimated current value	540,000
Paper profit	$175,000

In one year, Arlene had nearly doubled her original $200,000, at least on paper (in terms of equity appreciation), by converting the Moonlight Motel to office space.

Comparing Alternative Investments

Was it a good investment for Arlene? She certainly thought so. Some of her friends, however, pointed out the following: During the year that Arlene worked feverishly to get zoning approval, the price of office space *in the area* zoomed from roughly $1.00 per foot to about $1.20 per foot (a big jump of 20%). That jump meant that anyone who purchased *any* office building a year earlier, assuming they hadn't overpaid, would have seen it appreciate enormously.

Assuming a price jump from $1 to $1.20 per square foot (and a multiplier of 12), let's consider the appreciation on a building with 6,000 square feet rented.

At $1 per square foot per month
6,000 square feet
× $1 per square foot
$6,000
×   12
$72,000 annual income   = $600,000 value
12% cap rate

At $1.20 per square foot per month
6,000 square feet
× $1.20 per square foot
$7,200
×   12
$86,400 annual income   = $720,000 new value
12% cap rate $120,000 increase in value

By this method, net income is directly related to value—as net income goes up 20%, so does value. Arlene's friends said she could have made $120,000, simply by buying any office building for $600,000 and then waiting one year while the rents increased. They pointed out that of the $175,000 profit she showed, only $55,000 was due to her efforts at changing usage; the rest had to be attributed to an increase in rental rates.

$175,000   Arlene's profit

120,000   profit realized by investing in any office
_____   building costing $600,000
$55,000   additional profit caused by her efforts in
            remodeling and changing usage.

All of which goes to show that there's money to be made in office buildings, either by changing the usage or by sitting on the property, *as long as rental rates go up.*

As we've seen, the income derived per square foot in office buildings, while still a function of location, is mainly a matter of supply and demand. The more demand, the higher the rate for virtually all space.

When Rates Come Down

Arlene sold her Green Valley Garden offices within 18 months of purchase, and it was a good thing she did. Seeing the demand for office space, developers began building. Two years after Arlene bought the motel, the Green Valley market was flooded with 13 new office buildings, totaling over 400,000 square feet of space. The price, which had risen to $1.25 a square foot, began to stabilize and then drop, as owners of new projects cut their rental rates to attract tenants. The new supply caused a surplus. Demand was no longer strong enough to fill the available supply, and, after two and a half years, the rental rate on office space was back down to $1.15 per square foot!

This illustrates one last phenomenon about office space vital to the astute investor—the supply is cyclical. Scarce supply and high prices are followed by periods of overabundance and falling prices, which are followed in turn by new periods of scarcity (when no one has built because of the previous surplus) and higher prices. Shortages typically last two to five years, because that's the lead time necessary to get new projects on-line (find the land, get approvals and build).

The wise investor in office space buys or builds at the end of one of the oversupply cycles, just when a shortage is starting to develop. The idea is to jump in when the market is hot and get out when it goes cold.

Chapter Twelve

EXPLORING INDUSTRIAL PROPERTY AS A SMALL INVESTOR'S HAVEN

If there is one area of real estate from which the small investor traditionally has stayed away, it's industrial property. To the small investor, anything "industrial" sounded too sophisticated and complicated, or perhaps too arcane to get involved in. But that was a few years ago. Recently, more and more investors have been turning to industrial property as a safe haven—secure from rent controls and tenant organizations—that provides a "clean" investment. In the last few years, industrial property has seen perhaps the greatest growth in popularity of any type of real estate. And for good reason.

WHAT IS INDUSTRIAL PROPERTY?

Industrial property, basically, is any property with an industrial use. To put it another way, if it isn't retail or residential, it has to be industrial. This definition, however, now has only limited usefulness, because the distinction between retail and industrial properties has been blurring in many areas.

When most people think of industrial property, they think of a big old warehouse or manufacturing plant—of steel mills, oil refineries and auto-manufacturing plants. But those are the big uses of industrial property, which we will cover only sparingly in this chapter. Here we are concerned with the smaller, newer uses of industrial property—those which have allowed thousands of small investors to get into the field.

INDUSTRIAL PROPERTY AND THE SMALL-BUSINESS PERSON

Consider Arly. Arly was not a real estate investor; he was a businessman who did carpet and tile installation. Most of his business took place in someone else's home. Arly hired crews to install carpets and lay tiles. Until the crews went out, though, he needed a place to store his merchandise and equipment. He also needed an office where his secretary could answer the phone and take orders. Where could Arly find such a location?

In years past, Arly might have rented the back end of a retail store, located on a busy downtown street. As we saw in our discussion of shopping centers, however, today's major retailers no longer rely on busy streets for business; they rely on walk-in traffic in shopping centers. Further, the only back ends available in commercial buildings were located in the older down-town areas, and most of Arly's business was in the new suburbs.

Arly's choices were to rent a commercial store himself (which made little sense; he didn't need the storefront) or to buy a piece of property and put up a building (which he couldn't afford). Feeling that he really had *no* choices, Arly worked for a time out of his own garage, an admittedly poor arrangement.

The Industrial Park

Then, in an industrial area of town, an enterprising investor opened up a small *industrial park*—several rows of warehouse-like buildings, each one divided into smaller work areas. The investor was willing to rent out as much or as little space as any business person required.

For Arly—who wanted about 1,000 square feet to conduct his business, yet didn't want to pay retail prices for walk-in traffic he didn't need—it was heaven-sent. The industrial park owner charged only forty cents per square foot, less than half the going rate for commercial space. Not only that, the owner presented Arly with an essentially open area, which he could utilize in any way he wanted. Arly built several heavy-duty shelves to store carpeting and linoleum on, and he built in a small office. That's all he wanted—no frills, just a highly utilitarian area. It was perfect for him.

In the heavily industrialized and diversified economy of the United States in the 1980s, there are literally thousands of Arlys—small-business people who need to rent space at less than commercial prices. They are the service trade, and their need for space has been at least partially satisfied, in the last decade, by the industrial park. This is a multipurpose industrial building most often put up by speculative investors.

As we'll see, the return to investors on such projects has been enormous. But first let's consider other uses of industrial parks, such as the one in which Arly rented.

Many such parks are quite large, with hundreds of thousands of square feet spread out over dozens of buildings, and they generate their own kinds of business. (Because industrial usage is the heaviest type of zoning, commercial usage is commonly allowed within an industrial zone.) Small duplicating services, for example, often rent space and do storefront business. Small restaurants, catering to the needs of those who work in the park, also spring up. And, since so many people come to these industrial parks, some retailers establish outlets there. Typically, these are discount houses that depend on their advertised prices (not their storefront appearance) to drag customers in. Finally, these multipurpose, industrial buildings are used by professionals—such as typesetters, commercial artists and writers—in addition to their use by retailers and small industries.

INDUSTRIAL PARKS IN THE 1980S

As we move into the mid-1980s, more and more people seem to be turning away from conventional occupations—working for a large corporation—for reasons of freedom, age, health, or the inability to find work with a large company. Frequently, these people open a small business or go to work in someone else's small business. Whatever the reason, during the 1980s we are seeing a surge in the demand for small industrial space. And this surge is being turned into profit by investors who know how to take advantage of it.

How to Buy and Sell an Industrial Park for Profit

Cheryl had some money to put into a good investment. She wanted to try real estate, but she shied away from residential property. She didn't like the idea of having to ask families for rent money, and she knew she couldn't turn a family out into the street for nonpayment. On the other hand, she felt no compunction against throwing out a business person who couldn't pay the rent. Cheryl saw a wide line dividing business and residence, and on the business side, she was all business.

Cheryl talked to several brokers, and one suggested that she might be interested in a small industrial park which recently opened on the far side of the city. Cheryl was interested in any kind of real estate except residential, so she went for a look.

Mercer's Industrial Park had 15,000 square feet of space in three buildings, each containing 5,000 square feet. The buildings were brand-new, rented out to the first tenants for an average of thirty-five cents per square foot (an income of $5,250 per month), all on net leases. Expenses, including management, came to about $1,000 a month—leaving a true net income of $4,250, or $51,000 annually. The owner was asking $600,000 for the whole park.

The broker said that it appeared to be a good price. Relating net income to price, the return was 8.5%.

$$\frac{51,000}{600,000} = 8.5\%$$

Cheryl was interested, but she wanted more information on such things as the length of the leases. The broker had a breakdown of the leases in a schedule, which showed who the tenants were, what they paid per square foot, how many square feet they had leased, and for how long. The average life of the leases was nine months.

The Short-Term Lease

Cheryl thought again, then said, "It strikes me that with short leases like this, whoever buys this property will have to be rerenting within a year. At that time, if competing parks have opened, many of the tenants may simply move out to get the benefit of newer property."

The broker smiled and said that was not the case. In industrial property, unlike residential property, the tenants were basically interested in space. Newness of the property (as long as competitive buildings were just a few years apart) was not really a factor. The hassle and cost of moving kept most tenants where they were. "Remember," he said, "most industrial tenants have a lot of equipment, a lot of inventory, or both. They don't want to move unless they have to."

Cheryl agreed with his logic. "So short leases are no particular disadvantage," she commented. "These tenants probably will want to stay here."

"It's better than that," the broker beamed. "The short leases are a big advantage! Once these people are in, they won't want to move, and in a year you can raise the rents. As long as you don't go too high, they'll stay put. In a few years, they'll be paying far higher rent than today, and you'll have significantly increased the value of the property."

Cheryl felt that there was something wrong with that argument, but couldn't say what. By now, she was strongly interested in the property, but the price still seemed awfully high.

Getting the Best Price

'I have only $50,000 to invest," Cheryl said. "Can I buy this building with that much money?"

The broker's smile dropped. "It will take at least $200,000 to get in here," he said.

Before he could continue, Cheryl interrupted. "Well, I have three friends who also have $50,000, and we're going to get together to form a limited partnership. My attorney's setting it up."

The broker's face lifted. "Maybe you can get in, after all," he said. (See Chapter 5 for a further explanation of syndication.)

After her lawyer had set up the syndicated partnership, and she had evaluated the profit potential of the property, Cheryl offered $500,000 for the park. The owner accepted. Cheryl was excited.

Problems

Her first big shock, however, came with the short-term leases the broker had said were a big advantage. It turned out that many of Cheryl's twenty tenants had short leases because they had risky businesses. Hardly a month went by that one of them didn't fail. That meant Cheryl had to re-lease and clean up whatever mess the former tenant left. She had an agency handle the leasing, which cost money, not to mention the vacancy period.

Cheryl had learned her lesson. She insisted that new tenants rent for at least three years, have good credit, and pay on an escalating basis—thirty five cents the first year, forty cents the second, and fifty cents the third. It turned out that, at the time, there was little other industrial space available in Cheryl's area. Consequently, she found tenants readily available. (In industrial leasing as in mobile home parks, perhaps the most critical factor is the absorption rate—how fast you can fill up your building—fast-absorption rates means lots of income and the ability to meet mortgage and tax payments; a low rate means lots of vacancies and trouble.) Within a year, the building was fully rented on strong leases, and Cheryl felt terrific. "Nothing can go wrong now," she told her partners.

Unfortunately, that wasn't the case. After two years, her tenants were bound by their leases to pay a big jump in rent—from forty to fifty cents per square foot. By then, however, a lot of competing industrial parks had opened. Cheryl didn't worry; after all, she had leases.

But, suddenly, her tenants began breaking their leases. Some simply moved out; others noted some minor problem as the reason for breaking the lease. Cheryl found that, in order to force tenants to comply with their leases, she had to take each one to court. In addition, she could only sue them for the rent as it came due! (In some states, it is possible to sue for the entire amount.) The value of the leases suddenly came into question.

Eventually, Cheryl learned that the easiest way out was to compromise. She reduced the third-year rents to forty-seven cents, providing the tenants signed new, three-year leases with rent jumps in them. Her tenants stayed with her. Cheryl had learned another important lesson about leases.

Getting Top Dollar at Sales Time

After managing the property for 26 months, Cheryl decided to sell. Her monthly income, at $.47 per square foot on 15,000 square feet, was roughly $6,000 ($7,050 less $1,000 in expenses), about $72,000 per year. Using a multiplier of 12, Cheryl came up with a sales price of $864,000. She had strong leases (with escalation clauses) and sound tenants. She had no problem selling.

Cheryl had more than doubled her money in just over two years in an industrial building. In another two years, she would have more than tripled it.

If you think that Cheryl's return was unusually high, please be assured that it wasn't. From 1975–1980, the rates of return on inexpensively bought, well-financed, and well-run industrial parks, averaged over 30% per year! (By return, here, I mean actual dollar return on investment after sale, not annual return.)

Of course, by the mid-1980s, the rules may be different. If we continue to have reduced rates of growth, we may see a dramatic lowering of the returns from such parks. However, with well-financed, well-priced and well-managed parks, returns far higher than with other types of investment should continue to be possible.

SPECIAL PURPOSE PROPERTY

In addition to the multipurpose industrial park we've been discussing, another type of industrial property has been heavily built in recent years—the special purpose building. Usually, this is a large warehouse or plant built to suit one, very large tenant, such as a rubber company. I've seen one building in Colorado that devoted over 400,000 square feet to just such a use.

I don't recommend such property for anyone new in the field—the problems and risks are simply too great. In the building in Colorado, for example, the company went broke in the fourth year of the lease, and the property owner could no longer collect rent. Worse, since the building had been specifically designed to manufacture tires, it was extraordinarily difficult to find another tenant who could use it, and it sat vacant for nearly a year.

The problem with large, special purpose, industrial property is that it usually has only one tenant, and with a single tenant the landowner is at risk. After all, you can't get rent out of a bankrupt tenant any more than you can get blood out of a stone.

FINANCING INDUSTRIAL PROPERTY

In the 1980s, it seems that the key to all types of real estate investment is to get the right financing. With good financing, anything seems possible; without it, we can't go anywhere.

Industrial investment financing is not much different from commercial financing, in that there are both large and small lenders. The large lenders include insurance companies, pension funds, and financial institutions such as banks. The smaller lenders (those who will lend on smaller projects) include banks and some insurance companies who make loans through mortgage bankers.

These lenders generally look at two things when considering loans. The first is the tenant, particularly with a single-tenant property. Lenders want to be sure that the tenant is financially strong enough (unlike our tire company) to continue making payments during hard periods. Without a strong tenant, it's virtually impossible for an investor to finance a special purpose industrial building.

Secondly, lenders look at the property itself, particularly in the case of a small, multipurpose industrial park, such as the one Cheryl bought. Where tenants come and go, lenders are less interested in the tenants than in the potential of the property itself. In such cases, they are concerned about the property's location, its competition, design and management.

Lease-Back

A third kind of financing is sometimes available and can be of great advantage to the investor who can find it. It occurs when a company that owns land—on which it has built, or intends to build, an industrial building—needs to raise cash for the business or the building. The company finds an investor to purchase the land, and agrees to lease the land and building back, often for a long period of time. Advantages accrue to both the investor and the company. The company raises cash, yet retains its industrial location. The investor puts up cash for a presumably strong tenant.

The catch, of course, is the price of the property and the terms of the lease. A strong tenant, with a legitimate reason for raising money, will usually ask a reasonable price for the property and pay competitive terms on the lease. Some companies, however, are on the brink of financial collapse and are looking for any way out. To sell and lease-back property they own looks very appealing. The advantages to such an ailing company—principally the large infusion of cash—are great.

To the investor, such a sale and lease-back is very risky. A new infusion of money may not be able to save an ailing company. It could go out of business or simply take the money and not honor the lease. In either case, the investor would be stuck with single-tenant, special purpose property that might be very difficult to re-lease.

It's usually not too difficult to tell the good lease-back deals from the bad ones. In addition to a reasonable sales price and a competitive rent, a strong lease-back includes a good financial statement from the company (an examination of its books by a CPA is a necessity).

Bad deals seem to be a function of investor greed and the fact that sales price is based on rental income. What happens is that the company agrees to pay an inflated rent (with no intention of honoring the lease, it cares little what rent it agrees to), in order to jack up the sales price. And the greedy investor, who looks only at the high rent, usually gets stung on these deals.

Industrial property in the United States, during the 1980s, promises to be a shining star in the real estate field. And, as we've seen here, it's not nearly as hard to get involved in as it appears on the surface. If interested, you can begin by talking with agents and checking advertisements for local industrial property. Finding a good broker who specializes in industrial land will be a big help. Also, check with your accountant and attorney. These professional people often know of deals that are being made and can steer you to other investors with similar interests.

Chapter Thirteen

OTHER REAL ESTATE INVESTMENTS

For those of us who just don't want to get out of our armchairs, the opportunity has recently arisen to invest in real estate as a lender. As I've often noted in this book, finding money to borrow has become the single biggest problem for real estate investors in this decade. Providing a solution to that problem can sometimes mean big profit to individuals.

LENDING MONEY ON REAL ESTATE

Today, all across the country, there are firms which cater to the person who wants to lend money on real estate, but who doesn't want to get personally involved. These firms say, "Invest your money with us, and we'll find borrowers. We'll be sure the property is worth more than the amount of the loan. We'll handle the paperwork, collect the payments, and mail you the interest. You just put in your money and collect your profit." With returns running about five percent over the prime bank rate, this is an appealing investment.

But is it a good investment? Does it make sense?

Yes and no.

First we should understand that lending money on real estate is a higher risk investment than, say, putting our money in the bank.

The banks are guaranteed (in most cases) and liquid, which means that, even if they go broke, we can always get our money back. Not so in real estate. If a borrower defaults, we have to sell the property to get our money out, and the sale may or may not cover the mortgage. And what about those uninsured homes destroyed by landslides, hurricanes or earthquakes? It's the lender, not the owner, who takes the financial beating. Additionally, we can get our money out of a bank whenever we want. In real estate, however, it takes time; and if we want our money immediately, there is almost always a penalty or discount, which in some cases can be substantial.

Now let's talk profit. Any time we lend money at a fixed rate, we're assured that our return will never be less than the amount agreed upon, assuming the borrower doesn't default. If the rate is 15%, we'll get a fifteen percent return—no more and no less. If we invest $50,000 at 15%, we know we'll have about $57,500 ($7,500 in interest) at the end of a year.

But is that what we really want to do with our money? If we had invested the $50,000 in real estate, leveraged 4 to 1 (our property cost $200,000, and we borrowed the other $150,000), and our property went up in value by 15%, our return would actually be $30,000 on the same money!

$$\begin{array}{ll} \$200,000 & \text{property value} \\ \times \quad .15 & \text{assumed appreciation} \\ \hline \$ \ 30,000 & \text{profit (on paper)} \end{array}$$

Invest in a second mortgage and make $7,500, or invest directly in property and make $30,000. Which would you choose?

Surprisingly, many people prefer the mortgage. It is, after all, a clean deal. There's no property to find, buy, manage and sell—no headaches. And, depending on the rate of inflation, a 15% return might not be too bad.

Going Through a Mortgage Broker Versus Lending It Yourself

One inducement to having a mortgage broker (whom we'll call the mortgage company) handle our money is that it frees us of any bother. There are, however, some problems involved.

Will the mortgage company, for example, be one hundred percent certain of the property's value? When we invest our own money, we're going to be darn sure that the value is there; but when we invest someone else's, just how careful will we be? We'd want assurance from a mortgage company lending our money on a "second," that they would only loan a specified percentage of the true value of any property. Typically, such companies assure their clients that loans are based on only 75%–80% of market value. The 20%–25% margin guarantees that, should there be a default, the property can be sold and the money returned. That all depends, however, on the appraisal. Who appraises the property? The mortgage company itself? Security comes from an independent appraisal. When institutional lenders go through mortgage bankers, they *always* insist on independent appraisals, never relying on the mortgage company's determination of worth.

Is the mortgage company raking off a big chunk of profit that should go to us? Consider that the mortgage company makes the loan, services it, and we get the interest. Doesn't that sound a bit odd? Are mortgage companies altruistic? Are they doing all that just to do us a favor?

Mortgage companies usually make their money on points (one point equals one percent of the loan amount); though many also charge a nominal fee, usually ½%–1%, for servicing. On second mortgages, the points typically run from a low of 5 to a high of 25. That means that the mortgage company is charging the *borrower* an additional 5%–25% of the mortgage just for placing it. As clients of the mortgage company, do we see any of that money, or does it all go into the mortgage company's pockets? On the other hand, if we want to lend money on real estate by ourselves, are we prepared to do it? Doesn't the mortgage company provide an invaluable service?

They provide a service; it's certainly not invaluable. Mortgage companies find borrowers, but so can anyone else these days, with a classified ad in any newspaper. Mortgage companies make sure the property is worth more than the loan value, but so can anyone else, by using the yellow pages of the phone book to hire a competent appraiser. Mortgage companies service loans; so will most banks and savings and loans—without charge—if you have money in an account with them. Mortgage companies handle documents; so will any title insurance company or real estate attorney, and they'll help if and when it's necessary to foreclose.

So who needs a mortgage company? My feeling is that, if I want to lend money on a second trust deed on real estate, I'll do it myself. (*Note:* The novice shouldn't try this without help. Each state has special laws relating to real property. Have a competent attorney prepare your papers, to be sure that you're protected and in compliance with all applicable laws. Also, if you're totally new to real estate and have little idea of value, the aid of a competent real estate broker can be invaluable.)

THE SANDWICH LEASE

This is a sandwich unlike any you've ever seen. It's quite simple to understand but extremely difficult to put into practice. The sandwich lease occurs in the following way.

An enterprising individual, we'll call him Josh, finds a piece of commercial or industrial property that would make a great site for a warehouse, retail store, or whatever. Instead of buying the property, however, Josh *leases* it from the landowner, promising him so much now (usually a few months' rent) and so much a month (often on escalating terms) for twenty or thirty years. After that time, any buildings erected on the property will belong to the landowner. It makes for an alluring offer. Then our enterprising friend locates a suitable retailer—a furniture store, supermarket, savings and loan, or whatever—and leases the property to this tenant (sometimes even agreeing to build-to-suit).

What is the real estate position of our entrepreneur? Josh has leased the property *from* the landowner and then leased it *to* the retailer. He is *sandwiched,* so to speak, in between the two leases. But where does Josh's profit come from? That's the simplest part. We'll assume he leased the property from the landowner for $1,000 a month, then leased it to the retail outlet for $1,500 a month. He keeps the difference—$500 per month.

What's so great about $500 a month? Josh gets that money every month, every year, for the term of both leases—perhaps thirty years. And, if they're net leases with escalation clauses, the amount he receives increases monthly. While one month's profit may not be very impressive, over thirty years that $500 is worth $180,000, even without ups. And remember, Josh's initial investment was only the first few months' rent on the lease. (In the case where Josh puts up a building, he gets a mortgage and charges higher rent, and the rent differential covers the mortgage payment.)

What could be sweeter? Indeed, very little. The sandwich lease, where properly applied, is one of the most highly leveraged, real estate transactions. It involves the smallest investment, yet gives the greatest return over the years. The problem, of course, is finding both the right property and the right tenant.

In our example, we assumed a terrific location for the property. But if that were true, why did the landowner need Josh? Why couldn't he develop the property himself? The answer is that many landowners lack sufficient knowledge and so are hesitant to develop their own properties; yet they don't want to sell and thereby lose out on the long-term potential from good real estate.

After leasing the property, Josh still had to find the right tenant. And today, particularly with smaller properties, many retailers are looking to lease directly themselves, or in some cases even to buy. After all, why should they pay Josh the middleman's fee? By going directly to the landowner, they could have leased the property for only two-thirds of what Josh charged.

Anyone trying to work the sandwich lease is competing with real estate people working for every major retailer, which makes it very difficult to tie up a good piece of property. It's also a matter of price competition. Our retailer may like a particular location but not be willing to pay *more* than competitive prices for it. On the other hand, our landowner may want to lease but not for *less* than competitive prices. If that's the case, where is the room for people like Josh to make a profit by sandwiching in?

Sandwich leases *are* happening all the time, all across the country. What we've seen here are both the advantages and the problems associated with them. In spite of the problems, however, enterprising individuals are finding, tying up, and subleasing good property, and making handsome profits. All it really takes is the perseverance to find the right opportunity.

THE UNIQUE INVESTMENT

Speaking of opportunity, one point which never seems to be emphasized enough in real estate is that every community— every area of the country—is unique. What works in New York may not work in California. Along these lines, I've recently met two individuals who found unique real estate investments. They were unique because they were peculiar to the areas in which they happened; I doubt that their success could be duplicated elsewhere. But the stories are worth relating, because they illustrate that unique opportunities await all of us, right in our own backyards.

The Marina

Stewart loved to sail so much that he bought his own sailboat and rode the waves in San Francisco Bay. He had a problem, however. He couldn't find rental space for his boat; there just wasn't enough marina boat docking to go around.

Many people would have complained, put their name on a waiting list, and let it go at that. But Stewart knew an opportunity when he saw one. He organized a group of friends and business people, secured city, county, state and water-commission approvals, then built a new marina. Needless to say, he did very well on his investment. He charged competitive if substantial rates, and all of his slips filled almost immediately. He found a unique investment in an area where no one else was looking, and he made a profit on it.

The Ski Resort

Ed loved to ski. He would drive two hundred miles to the big ski resorts in the Sierra Nevada, almost every weekend of the winter. He paid twenty dollars a day for ski-lift tickets and upwards of fifty dollars a night in motel costs. He wasn't rich, but at first he didn't mind the expense. It was, after all, his favorite sport.

But as Ed got older, the high cost began to bother him a lot, and he figured it was bothering others as well. So he decided to seek a cure, and in it he made a profit.

After considerable searching, Ed found an ideal plot of land for a ski area, seven miles off the interstate. It had long downhill slopes and plenty of snow in winter. The reason it had never been developed was money—the up-front cost of putting together a ski resort was phenomenal. And since the area usually made money only during winter, and then only during heavy snow seasons, few lenders would consider making the loans necessary to finance a resort.

However, Ed had a unique method of financing his ski area. Since the property was virtually useless in an undeveloped state, the landowner was willing to help with the financing. In lieu of cash, the owner accepted an interest in the future ski resort, on the condition that he would get his property back if the venture failed, subject to any mortgages on it. (Since the likelihood of high mortgages was great, it was a considerable risk.)

Then Ed contacted nine other skiers and soon had a group together who believed in the project. They formed a limited partnership syndicate, raised a considerable amount of money, and borrowed the remainder on a fifty percent (of value) mortgage.

The project took two years to complete, but when it was done they had a resort building with sixty condominium units, plus a chair lift and several smaller ski lifts. They sold the condo units to friends, relatives, and the general public, which quickly returned the money they'd invested, paid off their mortgage, and showed them a profit. Business was good, and because their area was off the beaten path, it remained uncrowded and thereby more desirable. Finally, since the partners each had a condo of their own, they had a place to stay when they went skiing, or to rent out when they didn't.

Needless to say, Ed was happy with a real estate investment that resulted in both profit and pleasure. It was finding a unique need and filling it that made the money. Ed's efforts were unusual, but opportunities are out there waiting for any of us to find them.

CONCLUSION

Where are you going to invest in today's market? How are you going to achieve financial freedom? What are you going to do to protect yourself against the double threat of inflation and unemployment? Where are you going to spend your money?

Let's consider it seriously. Here's a list of possible investments:

- Stocks
- Bonds
- Rental houses
- Treasury bills (T-bills) (and other government debts)
- Money-market accounts
- Gold
- Silver
- Commodities
- Agriculture
- Leasing
- Research and development
- Oil and gas
- Investment real estate

Of course, the list is not complete. But I suggest that you look it over carefully and consider what you know about each item.

How has the stock market performed in the last year? In the last five years? The last ten? What about bonds? Have you recently seen anyone jumping for joy over their profits in stocks and bonds?

How are people doing who have *recently* bought or tried to buy a rental house? Are those who bought houses to fix up and resell able to sell them? What about T-bills and money-market accounts? Will you really be making any money *after taxes, after inflation*?

Gold and silver have seen hard times in the recent past. Are they about to surge up? Or are they going to fall further? Do you want to take the risk? Commodities suffer most in a recession, and they require the greatest expertise. Ask yourself this question: "Have I ever known anyone who made a profit in the commodities market?" Studies indicate that eighty-five percent of those who speculate in commodities lose *all* the money they invest.

What about agricultural property or bare land? Do you know anything about raising crops? It's not easy to learn, and bare land tends to follow the housing-market cycle rather than the investment-real-estate cycle.

Research and development of new products, as well as oil and gas, do produce astonishing profits . . . for those who are successful. But each of these investments is a *crapshoot*. What if the product is unmarketable? What if there is no oil or the development well just doesn't come in?

The list could go on and on, but I think the point is made— in today's economy, yesterday's investments just don't work anymore. They don't make you money without great risk. On the other hand, after reading this book, I hope that you don't think the same of investment real estate. As we've seen, office buildings, shopping centers, conversions, mobile home parks, and industrial parks are still doing well.

Of course, investment real estate is not immune from recession, but its slumps tend to be geographical. Office space may be booming in Los Angeles and New York, but dead in Chicago. Strip centers may be doing great in Houston and Denver, but dying in Kansas City. The only way to tell is to investigate your own area—right now. (Rereading the chapters on office buildings and industrial parks will help you learn how to "read" an area for growth.) Find out what cycle each type of investment property is having in your own area, then jump on the upswing.

Investment real estate is where the smart money is going in the 1980s. If you want to be smart with your money, you'll take a good, hard, long look at it yourself.